Money, Banking, and Financial Markets

This innovative text offers an introduction to money, banking, and financial markets, with a special emphasis on the importance of confidence and trust in the macroeconomic system. It also presents the theory of endogenous money creation, in contrast to the standard money multiplier and fractional reserve explanation found in other textbooks. The U.S. economy and financial institutions are used to explain the theoretical and practical framework, with international examples weaved in throughout the text. It covers key topics including monetary policy, fiscal policy, accounting principles, credit creation, central banks, and government treasuries. Additionally, the book considers the international economy, including exchange rates, the Eurozone, Chinese monetary policy, and reserve currencies. Taking a broad look at the financial system, it also looks at banking regulation, cryptocurrencies, real estate, and the oil and gold commodity markets. Students are supported with chapter objectives, key terms, and problems. A test bank is available for instructors. This is an accessible introductory textbook for courses on money and banking, macroeconomics, monetary policy, and financial markets.

Dale K. Cline is a CPA in public practice, a CMA, a business owner, and an investor. He holds an undergraduate degree from Lenoir-Rhyne College and an MBA from Wake Forest University. While he has a wealth of business knowledge gained through his client advisory role, he learned much of what he knows about the economy through hands-on experience. Most recently, navigating his real estate investment and development business through the Great Recession provided him with unique insight into the way the banking system and the economy respond to stress. Viewing the meltdown from the dual perspectives of a CPA and a market participant prompted him to embark on a study of the lesser understood intricacies of the economy that culminated with the writing of this book.

Sandeep Mazumder received his BA in Economics from St. Catharine's College at Cambridge University. He earned his MA and PhD in Economics from Johns Hopkins University. His research and teaching interests include macroeconomics, monetary economics, international monetary economics, and time-series econometrics. Sandeep has focused much of his research on U.S. inflation dynamics and the Phillips Curve, and has published in journals such as the *Brookings Papers on Economic Activity*, *Macroeconomic Dynamics*, and the *Journal of Money, Credit and Banking*. He was a Professor in the Department of Economics at Wake Forest University for 12 years, where he also served as Department Chair for several years. Since 2021 he has been the William E. Crenshaw Dean of the Hankamer School of Business at Baylor University. In addition, he also is an Associate Editor of the *Journal of Macroeconomics*, a position he has held for several years.

Money, Banking, and Financial Markets

A Modern Introduction to Macroeconomics

Dale K. Cline and Sandeep Mazumder

**With Research and Writing Assistance
from Tina R. Lineberger, CPA**

Thank you for your commitment and
service to the Hankamer School
of Business!

Sandeep

Routledge
Taylor & Francis Group

LONDON AND NEW YORK

First published 2022
by Routledge
4 Park Square, Milton Park, Abingdon, Oxon OX14 4RN

and by Routledge
605 Third Avenue, New York, NY 10158

Routledge is an imprint of the Taylor & Francis Group, an informa business

British Library Cataloguing-in-Publication Data
A catalogue record for this book is available from the British Library

Library of Congress Cataloging-in-Publication Data
Names: Cline, Dale K., author. | Mazumder, Sandeep, 1982- author.
Title: Money, banking and financial markets : a modern
introduction to macroeconomics / Dale K. Cline and Sandeep
Mazumder ; with research and writing assistance from Tina R.
Lineberger, CPA.
Description: Abingdon, Oxon ; New York, NY : Routledge, 2022. |
Includes bibliographical references and index.
Identifiers: LCCN 2021046990 (print) | LCCN 2021046991 (ebook) |
ISBN 9781032170305 (hbk) | ISBN 9781032170268 (pbk) |
ISBN 9781003251453 (ebk)
Subjects: LCSH: Macroeconomics. | Monetary policy. |
Banks and banking. | Money.
Classification: LCC HB172.5 .C59 2022 (print) |
LCC HB172.5 (ebook) | DDC 339—dc23
LC record available at https://lccn.loc.gov/2021046990
LC ebook record available at https://lccn.loc.gov/2021046991

ISBN: 978-1-032-17030-5 (hbk)
ISBN: 978-1-032-17026-8 (pbk)
ISBN: 978-1-003-25145-3 (ebk)

DOI: 10.4324/9781003251453

Typeset in Times New Roman
by codeMantra

Access the Support Material: https://www.routledge.
com/9781032170268

Contents

Prologue

This textbook is derived from BANKING ON CONFIDENCE, A Guidebook to Financial Literacy, a book written for a general audience, authored by Dale K. Cline, CPA, CMA, MBA, and assisted by Tina R. Lineberger, CPA, CGMA. Sandeep Mazumder, PhD, later joined the endeavor to reimagine the book as a textbook for a global student audience.

Introduction

In our time, the curse is monetary illiteracy, just as inability to read plain print was the curse of earlier centuries.

This quote, from Ezra Pound, American poet and intellectual, sums up the inspiration behind this book. It was born out of frustration with the myriad conflicting stories, reports, and debates about the economy. Regardless of our stations in life, we are all affected by the economy at the local, national, and even global levels. And when we encounter so much contradictory information, we are left wondering just how it all really works. The average citizen has a difficult time overcoming monetary illiteracy. Although a wealth of information is available from books and media outlets, much of it is laced with political sentiment, and separating the wheat from the chaff, so to speak, is difficult.

This book is meant to offer the average citizen a fundamental understanding of how to think about the economic world in which we live and work from an everyday point of view. It covers basic macroeconomic and financial concepts from an intuitive viewpoint, together with some of the key theoretical underpinnings that accompany the concepts presented. It is for anyone and everyone who is optimistic, pessimistic, or just curious about the way the economy actually operates. It is written to be user friendly, and is of particular importance to undergraduate and graduate students in business and economics.

There are some nuts and bolts about how the banking system works, how the money supply expands and contracts, and how currency markets operate. We will draw special attention to a theory that explains how money is created in the economy, which replaces the hypothetical story that is found in most textbooks. Since economics is really about how people think about and behave with their money, what you will find in this book is mostly common sense. We truly feel that the terms and concepts described in this book are important for everyone to know—whether you are a business or economics student taking a macroeconomics or money and banking class, whether you want to know more about the economy, whether you work in

DOI: 10.4324/9781003251453-1

finance, if you want to make better personal financial decisions, or if you want to be a well-informed voter.

This is not an investment guide, though there is discussion of how to consider values as they relate to wealth creation. It is not a political discourse, but there are references to the role that the government plays in economic policy. Important global matters are presented within a relatively easy-to-understand framework, with explanations that apply economic concepts to daily life. Historical events, such as the Great Recession and the 2020 Covid-19 pandemic, are interwoven throughout the text in order to provide real world examples of economic outcomes. And while the illustrations used may relate to a specific time in history, the lessons to be gained are timeless. Ideally, the reader will be armed with new insight into the way the economy actually works, through both discussion and examples, thereby empowering them to make better decisions.

Economics is often referred to as the 'dismal science.' Coined by Scotsman Thomas Carlyle in the nineteenth century, the term was inspired by the theory of economist Thomas Malthus which proposed that human population growth would perpetually outpace availability of natural resources, resulting in a general state of inescapable misery. That does paint quite a bleak and dismal picture. Spring forward to modern times and consider that the economic reports that garner the most attention are those warning of some negative outcome. Again, the general outlook is pessimistic, casting a negative pallor on the study of economics.

The current generation of college students has come of age in a time of economic uncertainty, with reports of recession and unemployment the norm. Even older Americans have become accustomed to the political mistrust and gridlock that seems to be commonplace. Perhaps that has colored the perspectives of many Americans who view the economy with skepticism. Most of them probably have this view because they find macroeconomic concepts to be unwieldy and complicated. With its many moving parts and labels, it is intimidating for someone who is not well versed in economic terminology. Yet, it actually is quite understandable, and far from dismal, when explained in everyday language.

It is our hope that this book makes you view macroeconomics as useful, interesting, and intuitive, rather than dismal. Realizing that we can understand how the economy is likely to be affected by certain events or conditions, using that information to determine the appropriate course of action to take for our own economic security can empower us, and that is exciting. The goal of this endeavor is to improve monetary literacy for each of us who cares about the economy, increase our knowledge base, and inspire us with confidence in our own understanding, one chapter at a time. Let us begin...

Part I

How the economy works

Nuts and bolts

Leonardo da Vinci once said, "The noblest pleasure is the joy of understanding." It is with the goal of gaining greater understanding that we venture into the world of macroeconomics. Much like painting a landscape, we will begin with the basic framework and then add subject matter, one layer at a time, which will gradually build in the foreground, the horizon, the sky, and all the other details that complete the picture.

The economy is an ever-changing animal. If macroeconomic outcomes were completely predictable, it would be simple for economists to develop prescribed formulas to handle any situation. Because the economy is a function of human circumstances, there are no universal formulas to provide systematic solutions for each and every scenario that comes about. So, any study of the economy must consider the actions of people. That certainly adds a layer of unpredictability!

Much like politics, we all have different experiences and outlooks that color the way we view the economy. But the universal truths remain constant. There are basic facts that apply to any study of the economy and these facts provide the foundation upon which the following chapters are built. Adding individual interpretation to the facts allows each of us to apply our understanding in our daily decision making. And while we might each see things a bit differently, if we understand the universal truths, we will make better decisions.

This will not be an arduous journey. The chapters are presented in a way that will gradually introduce topics and provide background without belaboring the point. Think of it as a stroll down a meandering road. We will stop off at a few points along the way. We may spend more time at certain stops than at others and we will see new things as we go. But when we reach our destination, we will have gained new understanding. Hopefully, we will have enjoyed the scenery along the way.

DOI: 10.4324/9781003251453-2

1 Confidence, monetary policy, and fiscal policy

Objectives

1. To understand the basic premise of monetary policy, fiscal policy, and how both interact with confidence in the economy.
2. To learn how GDP is calculated.
3. To study an example of government taxation and the implications it has for the economy.

Suppose it is a beautiful spring day and you are standing in your yard, admiring your well-cut lawn. You could stand there and admire the whole lawn all at once, or you could pull out a single blade of grass and then examine it in fine detail using a high-powered microscope back in your lab. In a similar way, we can apply this logic to the economy: one can look at the economy as a whole, known as *macroeconomics*, or you can zoom in on particular markets or industries, which would be *microeconomics*. For the purposes of this book, we are talking about the economy from the macroeconomic perspective.

One can visualize the economy on a macroscale sitting upon three pillars: confidence, monetary policy, and fiscal policy. Those are probably not the first terms that come to mind when you think about economics, but they are essential components of understanding how the economy works at a macroeconomic level. A healthy economy cannot exist without these three pillars standing strong, supporting and reinforcing each other. Each plays an individual role but all of them must be present and working together to optimize economic growth, stabilize inflation, and fight unemployment. Improvements in productivity, innovation, and technology all rest upon the foundation of these three pillars that form the bedrock of the national economy.

Confidence

Of the three pillars, confidence is paramount. Such a simple word. Yet, it may be the most important ingredient for a nation's economic well-being. The other two elements cannot compensate for a lack of confidence and, without it, the economy cannot prosper. The 2020 COVID-19 pandemic-induced

DOI: 10.4324/9781003251453-3

recession is an example of this: monetary policy and fiscal policy had a tough time fighting this recession because confidence was so low. Why is confidence so important? It sets the tone for everything else, infusing a positive spirit that inspires the ability to overcome seemingly insurmountable odds. A sense of confidence fuels business innovation and encourages employers to hire young and exciting talent. It also gives us the momentum to go out and spend our money in the economy. Confidence is important for us at the individual level, as well as for policymakers at the national level.

Confidence is particularly crucial when we face adversity. Apple Inc—one of the most famous companies in the world—was at one time a business on the decline. 1997 marked the 12th consecutive year of financial losses for the company, which prompted them to bring co-founder Steve Jobs back to the firm. Jobs came in and announced a large partnership with rival company Microsoft, which injected much-needed investment into the company. History now tells us of the amazing innovations that Apple has since implemented, propelling them into being one of the most iconic brands on earth. Lego is another great example of a company that has overcome adversity: their toys are now ubiquitous all over the world, but this was not always the case. In 2004, the company had a loss of $174 million and was on the brink of bankruptcy. That same year, Jorgen Vig Knudstrop became the CEO and immediately altered the business, including the goal of targeting movie franchises for their products. This helped turn around the company's fortunes, and today Lego is a household name all over the world.

To see the importance of confidence another way, see Figure 1.1 which displays the index of consumer sentiment, where the data are collected by surveys conducted by the University of Michigan:

Each gray bar on the diagram shows where a recession occurred. Do you see any patterns emerge? We can clearly see that each time the consumer sentiment drops for several consecutive months, there is a recession. This is not purely a coincidence! Confidence inspires people to imagine a greater future; to learn and use new technology to create a better world.

Monetary policy

The second pillar, monetary policy, is simply the process of adjusting, on an ongoing basis, the supply of money in the economy, the availability of credit, and the cost of borrowing. The implementation of monetary policy falls under the authority of the Federal Reserve Bank. The Fed monitors a myriad of economic indicators and data which decision makers use to determine the actions necessary to maintain the appropriate amount of money in the economy necessary to meet its end objectives of relatively full employment and low inflation. Working directly with the banking system, the Fed plays a key role in the way the modern monetary system operates. Depending on its goals, the Fed will implement actions which encourage expansion of credit in an attempt to stimulate economic activity or they may discourage

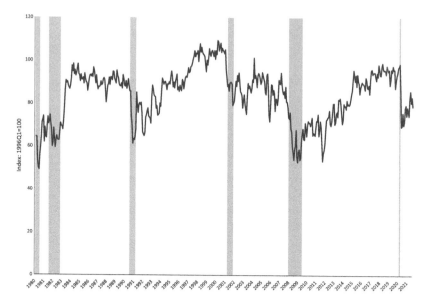

Figure 1.1 Index of Consumer Sentiment.
Source: University of Michigan

borrowing, thereby slowing growth. Hopefully, decision makers will achieve their goals most of the time, although it can be as much art as science. Using a variety of available tools, Fed authorities constantly seek to create the perfect balance in the economy which will allow it to thrive. It is not unlike Goldilocks' search in the classic fairy tale for the perfect porridge that is 'not too hot, not too cold, but just right.' And what is just right in one set of circumstances may spell disaster in another. With so many moving parts and an ever-changing fiscal environment, there is no single prescription to cure a particular ill. Monetary policy experts are constantly forecasting and attempting to make the most accurate predictions possible, as their decisions are the ones most likely to affect the economic lives of individuals. They carry a huge burden. Still, the obligation to get it right is not theirs alone, as monetary policy works alongside fiscal policy and the two must be well synchronized to create the best macroeconomic outcome.

Fiscal policy

Fiscal policy, which is the government's use of taxation and spending, is controlled by the government. The goal of fiscal policy is to control government spending levels and set tax rates in a proper balance in order to serve the private economy. It is probably the most well-known but least understood of the three pillars. Because it is carried out by way of the body of laws established by Congress, fiscal policy is often referenced in headlines and sound bites. Taxes are of particular interest because of their direct effect on each of us. Simply stated, taxation is the government's primary method of revenue collection. Fiscal policy seeks to balance that revenue with government spending and other regulations in a way that allows the private sector to flourish. Think of it as a tool kit. By adjusting tax revenues or budgetary spending, the government has the ability to implement changes directed at influencing and balancing aggregate demand, inflation, and gross domestic product (GDP). Historically, the portion of the private economy paid into the government through taxation was approximately 18%–20%. In more recent years, that percentage has been on a rising trajectory: the Organization for Economic Co-operation and Development (OECD) reports that the tax-to-GDP ratio was about 24% for the United States in 2018, meaning the government's size relative to the private economy continues to expand. Many believe that amount to be excessive because the revenue being funneled into a government program takes away from stimulating the private economy. Others believe that large government programs make such a great contribution to the well-being of the citizens that, to them, paying higher taxes is a justified way to redistribute wealth. Further, government spending does pour money into the private economy when it is being used to purchase goods and services for government projects, and there are theories that support the idea that deficit spending is a worthwhile stimulus for a sluggish economy.

While there are differing economic theories and opposing viewpoints, all agree that fiscal policy does have an impact on the health of the economy and it is clear that, to maximize its effectiveness, it must be executed in concert with monetary policy. Some argue that the role of monetary policy should be secondary to that of fiscal policy while others maintain that, when it comes to government regulation, less is more. Many believe that the government should provide the regulatory framework and then step out of the way, allowing the economy to thrive without the suppression of excessive governmental bureaucracy. Regardless of political leanings, all would agree that governments are necessary to create a balanced playing field and to protect property rights.

GDP

The previous discussion referenced the term GDP. An acronym for Gross Domestic Product, it is frequently used in economic discussions, but many do not really understand what it means. Why do we monitor GDP? How is it calculated? And why is it considered one of the most important measures of the economy's health and citizens' standard of living?

In a nutshell, GDP is simply the market value, in U.S. dollars, of all officially recognized final goods and services produced within a country in a given time period. The word final, as used here, means that the value of a given good or service that is produced is counted at the point of completion of the good or service, and the various components and wages are already included within that final value. In other words, although a car might be comprised of metal, glass, tires, etc., the individual parts (i.e. the windshield, the tires) are only included once in GDP as part of the final production value of the car. If they were sold separately, as when you purchase a new set of tires for your car, they are counted because they are being sold for final use.

Although there are several methods for calculating GDP, each method produces approximately the same result. Understanding GDP is an important building block to understanding the macroeconomy, because it measures, in the broadest sense, the economic health of nations. Is the economy growing at a reasonable rate to provide relatively full employment for those able to work? Are we earning a gradual and continuously improving standard of living as a nation? Is the final GDP calculation for a given year the *real* growth of the nation, or is it being expressed in current prices at current dollar values, also referred to as nominal GDP, without an adjustment for inflation? All of these questions hinge on a basic understanding of GDP and its role in measuring the economy.

As we just stated, GDP is the market value of all officially recognized final goods and services produced within a country in a given period of time. While GDP is arguably the best measure of well-being we have in macroeconomics, it is not a perfect measure—there are several reasons why this is the case. First, only newly produced goods are counted within GDP. So, the purchase of a new car gets counted in GDP, but transactions of used cars do not. Second, work done in the household is not included in GDP. For instance, if I were a professional chef and cooked a fine-dining meal at home for my family, that meal's value does not get counted toward GDP. Yet, if I did the same thing at my restaurant and customers paid for the same exact meal, this would count toward GDP. Third, GDP also includes the *imputed value* of certain necessary services that are provided to society, such as the work done by police officers and firefighters. And finally, it goes without saying that certain economic transactions are entirely missed in GDP calculations, such as illegal transactions.

Balance

Thinking again about the image of three pillars, strong and yet flexible, we get a sense of the balance that is necessary for the economy to operate like a well-oiled machine. In a perfect world, these three supports would function in easy harmony, fluctuating as necessary to maintain a strong system in which the economy could flourish. But the world doesn't always work that way.

With decisions regarding monetary policy and fiscal policy being made within the political arena, confidence can be elusive. Politicians debate and legislate and sometimes progress occurs extremely slowly. The resulting public frustration can lead to a lack of confidence in those decision makers and that can translate into fear for our economic future. Confidence can also hinge on the outcomes of elections, where the shifts in ideology can swing the pendulum back and forth, with fiscal policies changing in response. A properly functioning economy requires monetary policies and fiscal policies that work in harmony toward a common goal. Policies may change, but, ideally, the goal should remain steadfast. And, through it all, confidence must remain, or the balance will falter, and the economy cannot thrive.

So, with balance in mind, let's revisit the question that we touched on in the discussion of fiscal policy. What is the proper balance between the public and private sectors? This tug of war is often the root of political polarization, thrusting the debate regarding the balance of power and money between the government and the people into the heart of many fiscal policy decisions. It is an age-old question, the answer to which plays a pivotal role in fostering confidence in our elected officials and, thus, our economic future. Is there a point of equilibrium that maintains a necessary amount of government activity while fostering growth in the private sector and, therefore, a healthy overall economy? Sometimes, words such as *bigger government* and *deficit spending* have a negative connotation. And while many do not understand all of the inner workings of the banking system or the money supply, the average citizen does understand income taxes and the impact on his or her wallet. Yet, it is really all part of the same interplay between monetary and fiscal policy.

Consider this example:

If a relatively well-to-do individual is earning $200,000 per year at a 20 percent tax rate (with that 20 percent as an example of a rate close to the overall percentage of government revenue to GDP, historically), then they would pay around $40,000 per year in taxes, resulting in $160,000 of discretionary income. Now assume that they spend $100,000 on daily living expenses, things such as food, housing and transportation. The remaining $60,000 is now available for additional consumption or savings and investments. If used as investment, we can imagine that this money goes towards businesses that will generate future dividends and capital gains. So, as that $60,000 comes out of their pocket, it goes into fueling economic growth by financing successful existing companies, or innovative new companies, that will employ that capital to invest in new facilities, new technology, hire new employees, and produce newer and more efficient products. The economy is better off, and our investor will hopefully be rewarded with dividends and value growth on their invested money. Now assume that instead of a 20% tax rate, our citizen pays taxes at a rate of 30%. An additional $20,000 of their income will go to the government and they will only have $40,000 available for investment. The government now has an extra $20,000 to spend on public services, welfare programs, defense, domestic and foreign aid, and all of its other functions. Is the country, as a whole, better off financing these government programs or putting that money to work in the private sector? Some believe that when we allocate funds to the public sector, it eliminates the opportunity for that money to be used to fuel economic growth. They argue that the government is *crowding out* the private sector. Aside from the impact of a larger government on the economy as a whole, the funds injected into the government are used to finance bureaucratic jobs and federal programs, which some believe are acting to over-regulate the economy. In some cases, the workers who fill government jobs could perhaps be better employed, for themselves and the economy, in the private sector. So, when we speak of the government *crowding out* the private sector, we are talking about more than an increase in government borrowing and spending. And, while these are economic questions, there are strong political undercurrents which complicate the issues and sometimes create anger or fear instead of confidence and inspiration.

So, are lower taxes and less government always better for the private sector? What if the government only funneled its expenditures into productive programs and infrastructure? Is the $20,000 from our example better utilized by the government to carry out its functions or invested in the private sector, which is the driver of the economy? Which produces the better result for the citizen and for the country? Of course, this can, and often does, become the center point of political debate. While it may be compelling, it is not within the context of this book to make those arguments. This is a discussion of economic understanding, and in that spirit, we will disregard political viewpoints and seek to focus on gaining understanding of the way the economy works. In economics-lingo, we would refer to this as making *positive* statements that are based on objective facts, rather than *normative* statements that are made on opinions.

Think about how far our economies have come in just a couple hundred years: growth and innovation are simply astounding. Take the 2020 pandemic as an example: in less than a year from the onset of the Covid-19 virus, several pharmaceutical firms from all over the world had developed, tested, mass-produced, and distributed vaccines for individuals globally. The speed and scale of this operation was most impressive, particularly given how much damage this pandemic did to our global economy. The key to making the macroeconomy function, as we know, is balance. And, balance can be difficult to maintain when the three pillars are being tugged in different directions. Fiscal policies change from one administration to another all over the world, with monetary policies adapting in order to maintain equilibrium. That is the nature of governments and, viewed with historical perspective, it works pretty well—particularly in countries that are highly democratic according to most of the academic scholarship in this area. Policies aside, however, we can see that the most robust times were also the times when confidence was high. As time marches forward, we can only learn from past mistakes and hope to recognize obstacles when they arise, attempting to maintain balance and confidence into our future.

Key terms

- **Microeconomics**—the study of individuals, firms, and market behavior with regard to decision making and the allocation of resources.
- **Macroeconomics**—the study of the economy as a whole, with a focus on aggregate changes in unemployment, growth, and inflation.
- **Monetary Policy**—the process of adjusting the supply of money, the availability of credit, and the cost of borrowing.
- **Fiscal Policy**—the use of government spending and taxation to influence the macroeconomy.
- **GDP**—the market value of all final goods and services produced within a country in a given period of time.

End-of-chapter problems

1. Is the study of the following microeconomics or macroeconomics?

    a. Examining the pricing of airline tickets.
    b. Investigating the cause of recent unemployment.
    c. Forecasting inflation for next year.
    d. Determining what taxes should be levied on carbon emissions.

2. In your own words, describe briefly how a lack of confidence can be harmful to the economy.
3. Can the Federal Reserve try to stimulate the economy by spending more on infrastructure, such as improving our highways? Explain your answer briefly.
4. Suppose you are in the market for a new car.

    a. You decide to buy the brand a new Ford truck that was just manufactured this year. Does your purchase of the car count toward this year's GDP?
    b. Suppose instead that you buy a second-hand Chevrolet sedan from a used-car dealership. Does your purchase of this car count toward this year's GDP?

5. Let's assume a simple economy that is made up of just bread and milk. In 2020, the economy produced 10 loaves of bread and 50 bottles of milk. The price of a loaf of bread is $3 and the price of a bottle of milk is $2.

    a. Calculate 2020's GDP based on these data.
    b. Suppose in 2021 the bread price rises to $4 a loaf and milk prices rise to $3. Calculate 2021's GDP level.

    c.   Was the change in GDP from 2020 to 2021 a true sign of the economy's welfare improving? Explain your answer briefly.

6. Suppose an individual earns a salary of $100,000:

    a.   If the rate of income tax is 15%, how much after-tax income does the individual earn?

    b.   If the individual invests 30% of their net income, how many dollars is this?

    c.   Suppose the investment from (b) earns an annual rate of return of 5%—how much do they earn in one year?

7. Consider a government that wishes to invest in solar energy:

    a.   Name and describe two ways in which the government could indirectly promote firms in the solar energy industry.

    b.   What is a way that the government could directly promote firms in the solar industry?

    c.   Describe the pros and cons of each of (a) and (b), and which you would choose and why?

8. State whether the following are positive or normative statements:

    a.   Congress ought to lower income taxes.

    b.   Income taxes are progressive.

    c.   The Federal Reserve conducts monetary policy.

    d.   The Federal Reserve should conduct expansionary monetary policy when unemployment is high.

2 Basic accounting and financial statements

Objectives

1. Readers are introduced to accounting and its basic rules and principles.
2. This chapter also goes through some examples of T-accounts, income statements, and balance sheets.
3. A definition of *money* is introduced and explained, and two types of money are discussed.

Accounting is one of the oldest and most respected professions in the world. It is also the basis for understanding what makes the economy tick. It provides the framework that allows each and every economic transaction to be expressed in a systematic way. While much of the more complex accounting rules and regulations are beyond what the average person would wish to grasp, a basic understanding of the system is essential to understanding how the economy works. If a particular theory cannot be proven through accounting, then its validity could potentially be in question. And if a transaction cannot be expressed through an accounting entry, something is amiss.

Accounting, as we know it today, is based on a system called double-entry bookkeeping which was first codified in the fifteenth century by a Franciscan Friar named Luca Pacioli. While merchants and governments had been recording transactions in similar ways prior to this time, it was Pacioli who first described the system and, thereby, outlined the means by which all who used it should operate. It consisted of structured methods of entering transactions into journals and ledgers using debits and credits to affect the appropriate accounts. The system remains largely the same today, although there are myriad rules and regulations that serve to ensure consistency from one set of books to another.

Economic insight

What do you see when you look at a house? Perhaps the size of the house first grasps you, or perhaps the number of windows catches your eye. Or, it could be the color of the brick. What does not catch your eye is the mortar

DOI: 10.4324/9781003251453-4

that holds the brick together. Further still, you won't think about the nails and screws that hold the studs and joists of the house in place. Accounting is a bit like the mortar, nails, and screws of the economy—we may not see it at first, but it is the glue that holds things in balance. It enables us to record all monetary transactions in a way that we can measure what we have (assets), what we owe (liabilities), and the difference in those, which is capital (also known as wealth or net worth). We also record income and expenses with this system, which allows us to determine profit or loss for a particular period being measured. At its simplest, accounting allows us to understand the particulars of an individual's or company's financial position. However, we can use the same language that speaks to us about our personal or company's situation to also understand the broader economy. Accounting is essentially a doorway to economic insight, as it allows us to translate any set of financial data into a format that can be more easily compared, contrasted, and analyzed. And that common format lends confidence in our ability to rely on the data for economic decision making.

Perhaps most important for a study of economics, accounting allows us to understand the way the modern banking system works. Believe it or not, journal entries can tell the whole story. And because banking is the heartbeat of the economy, it is crucial to understand the role that banks play in the creation of money. Accounting provides us with the tools for that understanding. So, while it may seem bland or mechanical, accounting can open our eyes to the way the economy really works.

A user who is looking at an entity's financial statements or records, whether they belong to a business, a government agency, or an individual, should be able to understand them with relative ease because they were prepared using universal principles. The application of accounting rules and regulations matured along with the oversight that permeates the accounting profession today. That oversight sends a message of confidence to users of financial data, as it ensures uniformity of reporting. Consistently ranked among the most respected professions, accounting is typically viewed as being steady and somewhat safe. And while it may not be glamorous, the principles and regulations that are the hallmarks of the profession provide the framework for understanding how the economy works.

Debits and credits

It all begins with debits and credits. Each recording, or entry, that is made in our books, which is the common term used to refer to journals or ledgers, is entered in such a way that two different accounts are affected, debiting one account and crediting another, to fully describe the transaction. The debits are recorded on the left side column in a journal and the credits are recorded on the right. One way to think of debits is as the funds that are incoming into a household, firm, or organization, while the credits are what are outgoing. The total debits must equal the total credits, thus providing a framework for ensuring that transactions are *in balance*. As long as the proper types of accounts are debited and credited, then net worth, i.e. assets minus liabilities, can be properly determined. Two basic rules to accounting are simply that the accounts must balance and that every single transaction generates at least one credit and one debit.

Asset and expense accounts are considered debit accounts. Debiting these accounts increases them. Liabilities, Revenue, and Capital accounts are considered credit accounts. Crediting these accounts increases them. Here are some simple examples:

Assume this is the first year of operation for Generic Manufacturing Company.

If Generic sells a product for $100 in a cash transaction, the correct entry is:

	Debits	*Credits*
Cash (asset account)	$100	
Sales (revenue account)		$100

If Generic pays cash wages of $50, the correct entry is:

	Debits	*Credits*
Wages (expense account)	$50	
Cash (asset account)		$50

In the first example, the entry debiting the cash (asset) account and crediting revenue reflects the impact of the receipt of cash upon the sale of a product. Payment of an expense, as in the second example, is evidenced by debiting (increasing) the expense account and crediting cash, the asset, to reflect the expenditure.

When entering these transactions into a journal, the first step in the creation of accounting records, the debits are entered in the column on the left side and the credits are on the right. In our examples, cash comes into the checking account when the sale is recognized, therefore we debit cash and credit sales. Wages are paid from the cash account and recorded as expenses, so we debit wages and credit cash.

The activity for each account is maintained in the journal but it can also be expressed using a *T-Account*. Called such because it looks like a capital letter T, a T-account is a tool that accountants have long-used to quickly and easily keep up with transactions. This is just an alternative method of reflecting a transaction. While it is not necessary to use T-accounts, they sometimes help users visualize the entries. Some accountants prefer journal entries, while others use T-accounts for simplicity. Computerized bookkeeping typically operates in a journal format, essentially eliminating the need for T-accounts, but many accountants still prefer them when working out the proper accounting for proposed transactions or attempting to track adjustments to particular accounts. They may appear old-fashioned but they still work.

These are the T-accounts for the previous examples:

	Cash (Asset)		Wages (Expense)		Sales (Revenue)	
ENTRY #1	$100					$100
ENTRY #2		$50	$50			

After these two transactions, the company has $50 in cash ($100 sales revenue less $50 paid for wages). Whether looking back at the journal entries or the T-accounts, we can see that the company has recognized revenue of $100 and $50 in expenses, thereby producing a $50 profit. All obligations were paid so there are no liabilities. Since we know that net worth, or capital, is total assets less total liabilities, we can see that Generic's net worth is $50, which is the total of the assets ($50 cash) minus the total liabilities ($0). Notice that the debits are on the left of each column, the credits are on the right, and the total of the debits equals the total of the credits. Possibly the most basic of accounting principles, this is a truth that applies to every single transaction that is recorded. Regardless of the method used, total debits should equal total credits.

Having established that all transactions are recorded with this common format of debits and credits, we can take a look at several different types of entries. Cash transactions, such as those in our example for Generic Manufacturing Company, are usually the simplest entries. Other transactions may not involve any cash outlay or current income recognition at all. They may record a timing difference, such as a liability incurred for later payment of cash, or a receivable from customer credit sales which are booked before the cash payments are actually received. For example, if Generic Manufacturing decides to borrow money from a bank, the cash received is not income. It is simply money being borrowed now that will be repaid later. So, the company would record the loan by debiting cash and crediting a Loan Payable account. Although this entry does not affect company income or expenses, it is important in recording the borrowing activity and accounting for the cash being deposited now and repaid later, along with any interest expense incurred. Essentially, every financial transaction that occurs for a company, plus some non-cash, tax-related ones, must be recorded on the books in order to accurately reflect the company's financial position. Typically, many types of transactions will be booked during a reporting period, which may be any stated length of time, but is typically no longer than one year for most businesses. The ultimate goal for all of this accounting is to produce a set of financial statements, typically including, but not limited to, an *Income Statement* (sometimes called a Profit & Loss Statement or abbreviated as P&L) and a *Balance Sheet* (sometimes referred to as a Statement of Financial Position or abbreviated as BS), which provides users with a picture of the company's overall financial position as of the end of its reporting period.

An example of a basic Income Statement:

ABC Company

Income Statement

	Debits	*Credits*
Revenue:		
Sales		$100,000
Expenses:		
Wages	$50,000	
Material	20,000	
Overhead	10,000	
Profit		$20,000

An example of a basic Balance Sheet:

ABC Company

Balance Sheet

	Debits	*Credits*
<u>Assets</u>		
Cash	$20,000	
<u>Liabilities & Capital</u>		
Liabilities		$0
Capital (Retained Earnings/Profits)		20,000

These simple examples tell us the story that ABC Company started on Day 1 with nothing, and ended with $20,000 in the bank account, which represents all of its capital (i.e. profits). The Income Statement covers activity for a certain reporting period and the Balance Sheet covers the financial position at a stated point in time in the life of the business. For a helpful analogy, think of the income statement as a video that records over a period of time such as a year, while the balance sheet tells us the financial information at a snapshot in time, such as a photo taken with a still camera would. Considering that the balances on the balance sheet on the last day of an accounting period are still there on the first day of the next, it is easy to see that at the beginning of Day 1 of the second year, the Income Statement will start with zero transactions (because there hasn't been any activity yet) and the Balance Sheet will begin with $20,000 Cash and $20,000 in Capital. This recognizes that the profit or loss of each period is *zeroed out* on the Income Statement, and moved into the Capital Account on the Balance Sheet, allowing profit or loss for the new period to start over at zero.

The preceding discussion describes, in the simplest of ways, how a business, part of the private sector of the economy, accounts for its transactions. Although still operating under accounting principles and the double-entry bookkeeping system, reporting within the public sector, or government, is handled a bit differently. Accounting for private sector businesses focuses on reporting financial activity and, often, disclosing financial position for purposes of budgetary planning or shareholder reporting. For a governmental entity, where there is no profit motive, fiscal accountability is at the core of the reporting requirements. While budgeting may be a consideration, the primary focus is on compliance and disclosure. With public resources at stake, the entity is under an obligation to report its handling of those resources in its efforts to accomplish stated objectives. From a reader's standpoint, the financial statements will appear quite similar. Often referred to as Fund Accounting, governmental accounting revolves around the cash flows related to the entity or project in question. Typically, in lieu of a capital or earnings account, the balance sheet will reflect a net *fund balance*.

So far, we have viewed a simple company and the illustrations of its accounting entries and reports, but we haven't talked about the driver of this private sector company, which, at its heart, is the commercial banking system. Without banks to supply money, in the form of credit, to the economy, this company would operate much differently.

Money

What is money? It sounds like an easy question that most people can understand, but actually it does require some careful attention. In everyday language, we say things like "I made some money" or "that person has a lot of money." In macroeconomics, instead of using *money* in these sentences, the more appropriate words would be *income* and *wealth*. Money itself is the financial asset that fulfills three main functions. First, and most importantly, it must act as a medium of exchange. Dollars are only valuable in the sense that sellers will accept them for payment for goods and services from buyers. If you walked into a store and offered to buy something using some pebbles, the store owner would laugh you out of their shop! Other than the absurdity of it, this shows that the pebbles do not act as a medium of exchange, acceptable for payment. Second, money acts as a store of value. In other words, a dollar earned today can be used to buy products tomorrow or even next year. On the other hand, if we used milk as our form of money, this would not work because the milk will quickly spoil. Third, money must act as a unit of account that enables us to compare different prices. When you go online to buy a new pair of sneakers, the price will be listed in dollars. If instead, it said that the sneakers are sold for two shirts or three hats, that would be nonsensical. The unit of account feature of money does away with this. Without money and credit, we would return to a barter system, whereby citizens traded goods and services, which is what the world used prior to the evolution of the banking industry and the implementation of accounting principles.

In addition to the functionality of money, good forms of money often have desirable characteristics such as scarcity, portability, durability, divisibility, and uniformity. In history, we have seen two types of money: commodity money and fiat money. Commodity money is money with intrinsic value. This means the commodity being used for money has value itself. Classic examples are gold and silver, but other things have functioned as commodity money too, such as whiskey and tobacco, which have been used for money in the past. Alternatively, fiat money is paper money without intrinsic value. The paper our currency is printed on is not worth much by itself. The value lies in the fact that others accept it as a means of payment.

Accounting in the banking industry

Before we delve into how money is created and supplied into the economy, we need to examine the way the banking industry accounts for transactions and how that accounting system is reflected on financial statements. Though the accounting principles remain the same for general businesses and banks, their respective roles in the economy are quite different. When we think of a business, we think of a company making and selling shoes, a restaurant selling hamburgers, a developer producing and selling computer software, a doctor providing healthcare to us, a homebuilder building our home, a barber giving a haircut, etc. A bank, on the other hand, enables all of us, in our respective businesses, to literally *do* business. Think of banks as the grease that lubricates the cogs and wheels of the economy's financial mechanism. Besides processing our transactions and maintaining our deposits, it lends money to borrowers.

A typical bank's financial statements might appear something like this:

USA Bank

Income Statement

	Expenses (Debits)	Revenues (Credits)
Income:		
Interest Income		$200,000
Expenses:		
Salaries (Wages) paid to employees	$50,000	
Interest paid to depositors	50,000	
Other overhead	50,000	
Total Expenses	150,000	
Profit (Credit) or Loss (Debit)		$50,000

And, hypothetically:

USA Bank

Balance Sheet

	Debits	Credits
<u>Assets</u>		
Loans to Borrowers	$1,000,000	
Government Bonds	1,000,000	
<u>Liabilities & Capital</u>		
Deposits from Customers		$1,800,000
Capital		200,000
<u>Totals</u>	$2,000,000	$2,000,000

The point to remember is that, while the financial statements for a typical manufacturing or service business might look somewhat different than those of a bank, they both are based on the same basic accounting principles. Remember: Assets = Liabilities + Capital.......always!

The goal of this discussion of accounting and financial statements is not to build a full working knowledge of accounting but to lay the ground work, the platform, to allow us to move into a discussion of how money is created and supplied into economy. Accounting truly is the language of business. More than just debits and credits, it is the common foundation that allows for the communication of useful, relevant and reliable financial information. As such, when we look at the way the banking system works within the economy, we will rely on none other than basic accounting principles to understand where money comes from.

Key terms

- **Accounting**—the process of recording financial transactions.
- **Double-Entry Bookkeeping**—a system of accounting where every entry requires a corresponding and opposite entry, where the double entries are referred to as debits and credits.
- **T-Account**—an informal table used by accountants to visualize transactions that are formalized with journal entries in double-entry bookkeeping.
- **Income Statement**—reports the revenues and expenses for a firm over a given period of time.
- **Balance Statement**—reports a company's assets, liabilities, and equity for a specific point in time.
- **Money**—an asset that is accepted as a medium of exchange, acts as a store of value, and as a unit of account.

End-of-chapter problems

1. Suppose the Deacon Company sells an item of product for $250, where the customer pays by writing a check from their checking account.

   a. How does this transaction appear in the Deacon Company's debit and credit accounts?

   b. The Deacon Company also pays its employees $150 in wages. Record this transaction in their debit and credit accounts.

   c. Show how the transactions from (a) and (b) appear in T-accounts for the Deacon Company.

2. Consider ABC Company example from Chapter 2. ABC then makes an additional $50,000 in sales, which are received in cash, while paying an additional $25,000 in wages, $10,000 in materials, and $5000 in overhead.

   a. Show what the ABC Company's Income Statement now looks like.

   b. Record what the ABC Company's Balance Sheet looks like.

3 . Explain briefly the difference between an Income Statement and a Balance Sheet.

4. A small island nation makes a discovery of beautiful and precious stones that can be mined from under the earth and are rare to find.

> a.   Could these stones function as money on this island? Explain why or why not?
>
> b.   If the stones were actually enormous boulders, could they still function as money?
>
> c.   Continuing from (b), what characteristic of money do these large boulders not fulfill?

5. Suppose the Black and Gold Bank has $150,000 in interest income, pays its workers' salaries of $100,000 while having various overhead expenses, such as rent and utilities, of $75,000. Calculate their profit or loss from this period.

6. The Black and Gold Bank makes a total of $500,000 worth of loans to their clients this year and has $100,000 in capital. Write down what their Balance Sheet may look like.

3 Relationship of the Federal Reserve Bank and the U.S. Treasury Department

Objectives

1. To learn about the goals and tools used by a central bank, the ministry of finance, and the relationship between the two.
2. The specific relationship between the Federal Reserve and U.S. Treasury Department is examined closely.
3. Bond pricing is studied, both intuitively and mathematically.

Does the average citizen of a nation really understand what their central bank does? What about their ministries of finance? Some people may have a very basic understanding of what they do, but from our experience, the majority of individuals are not well-versed regarding the operations of these entities. In this chapter, we will examine this relationship further, and we will do so specifically by looking at arguably the most well-known and influential pairing of a central bank and finance ministry in the world, namely, the Federal Reserve and the U.S. Treasury Department.

The role of the Federal Reserve

The Federal Reserve, commonly referred to as 'the Fed,' is the central bank of the United States, the bank to the commercial banking system, and the *banker of last resort*. You can even think of the Fed as being the bank to the banks. Created by the Federal Reserve Act in 1913, the system is made up of 12 regional banks and 25 branches. Leadership is provided by a seven-member panel known as the Board of Governors. The members of the Board of Governors are nominated by the President and confirmed by the Senate. Interestingly, governors of the Fed have 14-year terms. This is not a typo—we said 14 and not 4! This may seem extreme on the face of it, but it's actually for a good reason. Namely, we want our central bankers to conduct good, sound monetary policy that forms a pillar of our economy, in order to bolster confidence. By giving them long terms, they can avoid the political pressures may exist in governments and can instead focus on doing monetary policy well.

DOI: 10.4324/9781003251453-5

Based in Washington, DC, the Board is charged with guiding and administering the activities and policies of the Regional Reserve Banks as well as providing broad oversight of the nation's financial services industry. Board members—particularly the Chair—are frequently called upon to communicate with Congress and provide updates to governmental leaders in regard to current financial conditions and the overall health of the economy. While these duties are certainly important, perhaps the most critical role that Board members fulfill is the interaction with and oversight of the Federal Open Market Committee (FOMC). All seven Fed Board governors sit on the FOMC. Of the remaining five seats of the FOMC voting committee, one belongs permanently to the President of the New York Fed, and the other four rotate among the remaining eleven district bank Presidents. Why does the New York Fed have special priority on the FOMC? It is because the Fed's open market operations are conducted by economists at the New York Fed. It is through the FOMC of the Federal Reserve System that the Board is able to implement and carry out its monetary policy, seeking to bring about stable levels of employment and moderate inflation.

Although many believe that the Fed is a governmental operation, in actuality, the Fed is an independent institution. While its shares are owned by its member banks, it is somewhat akin to a co-op in that ownership of shares is required for membership. Sale or transfer of the shares is restricted so they cannot be publicly traded, and dividends are paid at a set rate. The Fed's annual earnings are turned over to the Treasury Department, so shareholders do not benefit from any net revenues. Because the Fed is not operated for a profit, the shares do not hold an element of investment and there is no sense of control by or obligation to shareholders, attributing a sense of operational independence. Additionally, the Fed is able to make decisions and carry out its monetary policies without governmental approval, thereby making it independent. However, it is subject to Congressional oversight and reporting and there is always a possibility that Congress could enact statutes that would affect the powers of the Fed. Because the interests of the government and the Fed are so closely linked, the two often act in partnership, making the Fed somewhat of an agent of the government. So, while it functions with autonomy, it still operates under the shadow of the government and each administration does exercise a degree of influence over Fed activities. This arguably is seen most visibly when a President renews a Fed Chair's term, or alternatively nominates a new one.

The U.S. Treasury Department and its relationship with the Fed

The U.S. Treasury Department is not an independent entity by any means— it is *owned* by the American citizens. Created by an act of Congress in 1798, it is the department of the U.S. government that is responsible for managing the nation's money. The Treasury manages our government's accounts, collecting tax revenue, overseeing issuance of debt and paying bills. Since it is the *money purse*, you might say it runs the whole show. The Treasury carries out its many duties through branches that operate under the U.S. Treasury umbrella. One such branch is the Internal Revenue Service. Think of the IRS sort of as a collection agency for the Treasury. When U.S. citizens send in tax money they owe to the Internal Revenue Service, they are really sending it to the Treasury Department, where it is used to pay the government's bills. And since the Treasury is charged with collecting revenues and paying bills for the country, it has a vested interest in fostering a stable economy. That's where the Fed comes into play. Working together, the Fed and the Treasury carry out their respective duties to promote economic health. The Treasury manages the government's money and the Federal Reserve serves as the government's bank, processing transactions on behalf of the Treasury. Additionally, recall that the Federal Reserve is technically a non-profit institution, turning its profits over to the government. Between the Fed profits and the revenues collected by the IRS, most all federally mandated levies end up in the Treasury Department bank accounts at, you guessed it, the Fed. And that is from where it is disbursed. Whether it is for entitlement programs (think Social Security, Medicare, Medicaid, Welfare), National defense, resources such National parks, etc., the Treasury bank accounts at the Fed are *collection central*, and *disbursement central*.

Where does our money come from?

Most people know that the U.S. government authorizes the printing of Federal Reserve Notes, or dollars, and minting of coins. Other than the value of the materials used in the production of the money, it technically has no intrinsic value, and thus is fiat money as we have previously defined. We could just as easily be using furs or stones or shells, as in the past. But our system operates based on paper notes and coins that are assigned value based on their denomination.

Since we know that the U.S. Treasury is the arm of the government that manages our nation's money, it stands to reason that the responsibility for production of our money would rest with the Treasury. The U.S. Bureau of Engraving and Printing, one of the departments of the U.S. Treasury, is charged with printing paper money for delivery to the Federal Reserve. Coinage is minted under authority of another Treasury division, the United States Mint. Actual production of the currency entails a very complicated process designed to achieve such a level of quality that the notes and coins cannot be easily counterfeited. The Federal Reserve then purchases the cash from the U.S. Treasury at a given price, generally based on manufacturing cost in the case of notes and face value for coinage. The notes and coins are carried on the Fed's balance sheet as assets (debits) and the payment to the Treasury is made by crediting the Treasury's account at the Fed. The Fed then introduces the notes and coins into the currency supply by selling them to the eight regional Federal Reserve Banks at face value. That transaction is reflected as a credit on the Fed's balance sheet and a debit to the banks' reserve accounts. From there, it filters into the commercial banks and, eventually, into our pockets. The banks carry the currency on their balance sheets as assets so when we walk into the bank and withdraw cash from our checking or savings account, the bank credits its asset account and debits our account.

Seigniorage

But why is the currency sold to the banks and what about the difference in the amount the Fed pays for the cash and the price at which it sells it to the banks? Who is the beneficiary of that profit? If the Fed pays a few cents for a $5 or $10 bill and then sells it to the banking system at face value, there is potential for the Fed to make a tremendous profit. The term for this profitable sale of raw currency from the Fed to the banking system is known as seigniorage, and its value as a practice in our modern economy lies in the fact that the currency is merely an obligation of the government. Simply put, the coins and notes that we know as money are simply representations of liabilities of our government. They are given value based on what the government promises to honor in exchange for them.

The entire system is based on the fact that the government will only accept U.S. dollars and cents in payment for taxes. So, the value cycle begins and ends with the government. Therefore, the built-in difference in the face value assigned to units of currency over the cost to produce the money results in the seigniorage profits that ultimately benefit the U.S. Treasury. While the currency is purchased from the Treasury by the Federal Reserve in the process previously described, the Fed is simply a mechanism in the supply chain of currency to the economy, but it does not stand alone as a profit-making entity. Any profit from the sale of currency to the banks is returned to the Treasury, along with the interest paid on any Treasury Notes held by the Fed. Because these funds return to the Treasury, which is ultimately held by the U.S. citizens, it is the people who eventually benefit in the form of reduced taxes or an offset to government spending.

But policymakers worldwide need to be careful about seigniorage. While seigniorage is a way for a government to generate revenue, it must be used with caution. Later in this book, we will talk about how an excessively growing supply of money can lead to inflation. Indeed, history shows time and time again (such as in Zimbabwe in 2007) that countries that are overly reliant on seigniorage revenue for government spending almost always deal with hyperinflation, which is severely damaging to an economy. The peak monthly inflation rate for Zimbabwe's hyperinflation period was a staggering rate of almost 79 billion percent in November 2008, compared to the inflation rate of 2%–3% averaged by most advanced economies in the world. In the United States, seigniorage has tended to account for about 3% of government spending, and we have not had such hyperinflation episodes.

Budget deficits, debt, and government bonds

We often hear about the growing national debt and deficit spending but how many of us really understand how a ministry of finance funds a deficit? If disbursements exceed revenues, obviously, the difference must be financed. Note that the terms *debt* and *deficit* are related but are different. Simply put, the national debt is the accumulation of all the years of deficits and surpluses generated by the government. Deficits are handled on a continual basis when the Treasury anticipates a cash shortage and finances it through the sale of Treasury Bills (short-term) and Treasury Bonds (longer term maturities). These government bonds are debt securities, whereby people lend money to the government for an agreed period of time. In return, the government pays back interest disbursed at regular intervals (known as the *coupon payment*, which is why bonds are often called 'fixed income' assets) plus pays the face value of the bond back at the maturity date of the bond. The mechanism for doing so is through a network of primary dealers, which are securities dealers that the Federal Reserve has approved to participate in the initial issuance of government securities as well as the execution of ongoing trading activities with the Fed.

The list of the primary dealers, which is published and regularly updated by the Fed, includes 24 banks as of this writing. These dealers are selected through a bidding process and they are required to meet minimum liquidity and capital standards in order to remain on the list. These dealers contract with the Treasury to market newly issued bonds to banks (themselves included, in the case of primary dealers who also have banking operations), corporations, pension funds, individuals, etc., establishing the initial market for the securities. In addition, they maintain open communication with the Federal Reserve to provide information on current and anticipated market conditions in order to assist the Fed in developing monetary policy.

Primary dealers use an auction format to get Treasury securities (often called Treasuries for short) to market. Although Treasuries are only issued through the primary dealers, the mechanics are much like any other auction. Because the primary dealers are in tune with the market and their information is shared with the Fed, the issuance is a team effort of sorts, with the Fed directing rates and terms while the Treasury controls the volume being issued at a given time.

Bond prices

At this juncture, it is very useful for us to consider what determines the price of a government bond. To answer this question, we need to understand two concepts known as the *future value* and *present value* of income. While these terms sound complicated, they are actually very easy to understand. Let's begin with an example: suppose you are given the choice between receiving $1,000 in cash today, or $1,000 in cash tomorrow. Which one would you choose? Probably, it would not make a huge difference to most people if the choice was between today and tomorrow. Now, let's change the example: the choice is between $1,000 today and $1,000 in 10 years' time—which would you choose? The answer is probably obvious: most people would choose the $1,000 today. Why? With the $1,000 today, there are all sorts of things you can do with it for the next 10 years, besides actually spending it. In particular, you can earn interest on it by saving it in some sort of interest-bearing asset. Suppose you take the $1,000 and put it in a regular savings account which promises to pay 3% interest annually. After 1 year, you will have earned $1,000 × 1.03 = $1,030. After 2 years, you will have earned $1,000 × 1.03 × 1.03 = $1,060.90. After 3 years, you get $1,000 × 1.03 × 1.03 × 1.03, and so on, where the compound interest accumulates. After 10 years, that $1,000 has grown into $1,000 × 1.03^10 = $1,343.92.

To generalize this formula, any one dollar today will grow into $(1 + R)^N in the future, where R is the interest rate earned and N is the number of years in the future into we are projecting. Now, let us ask this: assuming the same interest rate of 3% as used in the previous example, how much is $1,343.92 in 10 years' time worth to you today? The answer is $1,000, because we just calculated that $1,000 now will grow into $1,343.92 in 10 years' time. From this perspective, the $1,000 is the present value of the future dollars that will be received. Mathematically, the present value of $1 in N years' time is worth $1/(1 + R)^N to us today. Notice that this number is a fraction that is smaller than 1. So, $1 next year is worth less to us than $1 today, because we could have invested that one dollar during the course of the year and made more.

Now that we have defined what present value is, we can understand bond prices. The bond price is simply the present value of future income that will be received. For instance, suppose a government bond is issued for 30 years, and pays a coupon payment of $C every year until the thirtieth year, whereupon the face value of $F is also paid. Assuming an interest rate of R percent, we apply the theory of present value to "discount" each coupon payment that is made in future years. This gives us a value of how much those future payments are worth to us now. The sum of all of these future payments (in present value terms) gives the bond price. Thus, the bond price is:

Bond Price = $C/(1 + R) + $C/(1 + R)^2 + $C/(1 + R)^3 +......+ $C/(1 + R)^29 + $(C + F)/(1 + R)^30,

where you will notice the face value is disbursed with the terminal payment. It is crucial to observe that bond prices and interest rates are inversely related in this equation: if current market interest rates fall, we should expect bond prices to rise, and vice versa. To see a numerical application of the above formula, assume the coupon payment was $50 each year and the interest rate was 5%, with a face value of $5,000: if we do the math, we get a bond price of $1,925.51.

While Treasury auctions are tightly controlled in terms of administration, the rates are still determined by the market. Let's assume the government is offering $10,000, 10-year bonds with a coupon rate of 6%. The market may be willing to bid only $9,500 for this particular issue. That would mean that the market believes that 6% is not sufficient yield (interest) for this bond and values it (bids) lower, achieving a higher yield (6%/9.500 = 6.3%). Treasuries are initially issued through this primary dealer network so that the entire market may decide the risk and reward ratio rather than the government itself.

If the market perceives that the government is spending too much and continually doing so by issuing more Treasury Securities to finance that spending, the market will demand an ever-higher yield, thus paying a lower price, for new issues of Treasuries. There are some differences in categories of bidders that allow more or less influence on the bidding process, but the important point is that, by offering the securities in an auction format, the ultimate control over rates lies with the market.

The role of the Fed in bond markets

While the market does indeed control rates, the Fed certainly plays a role. The Fed also may, in times of low national confidence, purchase Treasury securities in such great amounts, that remaining issued Treasuries held by the private sector are insufficient to satisfy existing demand. This demand versus supply pushes prices for these securities artificially high, and their corresponding yield artificially low. This can be true if the Treasuries have existed for some time or are newly issued, financing current deficits. These Fed purchases enlarge the commercial banks' reserve pool, lowering the Fed funds rate to encourage borrowing and, hopefully, grow the economy. And since a lower Fed funds rate—which is the Fed's target interest rate—raises the present value of future income, we should expect bond prices to climb.

Values of these securities still held by the private sector rise in response to reduced supply and their corresponding reduced yield tends to push up other financial assets' values held by the private sector. Of course, none of this is about economic fundamentals, but government intervention in the form of spending more, financed by Treasury issuance. Since the Fed is involved heavily in bond markets, this sometimes brings criticism of the Federal Reserve, as citizens who own financial assets appear to benefit while others do not. However, if confidence is restored in society and the economy begins to grow vigorously, the dilemma is self-solving. If confidence is not inspired, the economy may stagnate indefinitely.

Though governments occasionally attempt to spur economic growth through deficit spending, this practice may culminate in a situation where debt levels are high and growth rates low. While this is of concern, we should remember that government debt is mirrored by the private sector's savings, as bonds are just another way individuals, businesses, retirement plan managers and others store their wealth. The private sector has chosen to loan its savings in order to receive interest payments. And while we can question whether holding large balances in Treasury securities is just an example of government borrowing crowding out investment in the private sector, the fact remains that there will always be demand for the safe-haven securities. Still, the historically high national debt in many countries around the world is a reminder that monetary policy and fiscal policy must be in healthy equilibrium to inspire the confidence in their citizens that is critical to create continuous, well-balanced growth, as we do not want governments to overspend relative to GDP.

While equilibrium is certainly the goal, it is not simple to maintain. Just the word deficit causes concern. Many have an overall negative view of the government based on deficit spending alone. Indeed, many believe that our economies are in worse shape than our politicians claim. And if we believe the media headlines, we may be headed for catastrophe.

The Treasury is not like a business or even our individual households, where we have a limited amount of income and resources that must be balanced with our spending or we become insolvent. Because it has a unique position as the issuer of its currency, the Treasury can actually spend without regard to its income, financing its deficit spending by issuing debt or relying on the Federal Reserve to supply funds as needed. What does this mean? Simply that, if the government requires more funds, it authorizes the issuance of more Treasury securities.

What about the debt ceiling, you ask? Well, while it does limit the ability to issue more debt, it serves more of a political purpose than a practical one. The parties in government may blame one another but, at the end of the day, they will do what is necessary for business to continue as usual.

What happens when all of the debt becomes so large that the governments cannot meet maturity obligations? There is not likely to be a sudden shift in the market whereby Treasury holders demand to cash out. Most Treasury securities are rolled into new ones at maturity, so they really just continue on. And while demand does fluctuate somewhat, Treasuries are going to remain attractive as savings vehicles because they are backed by the government, making them quite safe.

If the market did suddenly move away from Treasury securities, the government would honor those obligations. Because the United States has a fiat currency system and the government directs the issuance of its own currency, it does theoretically have the ability to direct the Federal Reserve and the banking system to provide it with needed funds. Now, it would certainly be inflationary to do so, and we know that our system currently does not operate that way, but the option to avoid bankruptcy is there.

Not only is there a mandate for primary dealers to always participate in auctions of Treasury securities, but, with Congressional authority, the Treasury can also obtain direct funding from the Federal Reserve. While this would only occur in an emergency situation, it certainly is an available remedy if there was a time of crisis. So, the government will not run out of money unless it chooses to do so. It cannot go bankrupt because its spending is not constrained by solvency. However, the government cannot disregard the effect of unrestrained spending on the overall economy, namely infla-tion, which would be the result of funneling too much liquidity into the economy at a given level of productivity. The Fed must always keep its eye on the overall level of national debt relative to GDP. While many political debates make reference to the mounting debt being handed down to future generations to repay, the real concern should be the ratio of government debt to our national productivity.

Think for a moment about the concept of borrowing. Typically, we bor-row in order to accelerate the ability to afford something we want or need. In business, we borrow in order to grow productivity more quickly than we otherwise could. If that productivity is healthy, then the business will pros-per. In the case of government spending, if a country is leveraging wisely, using deficit spending as a way to grow GDP at a faster, but still healthy, rate, then the debt incurred is beneficial to overall living standards. As ad-vanced economies' levels of national debt have risen, so have their standards of living. Put another way, the thought of the government having trillions of dollars' worth of debt may sound scary, but that is not the relevant number. Instead, what is relevant is whether the growth of the debt is higher or lower than GDP growth rates. If GDP growth rates are higher than the growth rate of the debt, then we are getting richer as an economy and are producing more and should easily be able to repay the debt.

There will always be differing opinions on the validity of government programs and deficit spending and we will not optimize it all of the time. But historical economic success can be viewed as evidence that when defi-cit spending is funneled wisely into productive channels which permit the private sector to flourish, GDP will rise along with a country's average standard of living, benefitting current and future generations. If govern-ment spending is irresponsible, then we would expect to see living standards stagnate along with GDP. That is the burden that we do not want to place upon the shoulders of future generations.

So, rather than focus on the amount of government debt accumulating, which is the tag line used by politicians, we should pay attention to the ef-ficiency of the government's spending. Wise spending, such as beneficial infrastructure or defense spending that maintains global peace and pros-perity, will pay off for generations to come in terms of increased output which will improve the ratio of debt to GDP. And that brings us back to equilibrium. Once again, we see that the key to maintaining a healthy econ-omy is the balance of the three pillars that we discussed in the first chapter.

Clearly, the Federal Reserve and the U.S. Treasury play key roles in the way both the United States and global economies work. While technically independent of each other, they co-exist in such a way that they operate in harmony in an attempt to accomplish the overall goal of maintaining stability in our economy. Without one, the other would be less effective and the sum is perhaps greater than the total of the two parts. But, as impor-tant as their roles are, they do not, and cannot, act alone. As stated in the introduction to this chapter, our goal is to better understand the economy and we cannot attain that without a clear working knowledge of how the banking system operates. Having now developed a familiarity with the roles played by central banks and ministries of finance, we have laid the ground-work to move into a discussion of the commercial banking system and its importance in our economy.

Key terms

- **Central Bank**—a national bank that provides financial and banking services for its country's government and commercial banking sys-tem. They also conduct monetary policy by manipulating the supply of money.
- **Ministry of Finance**—the government department that manages the treasury and oversees the spending of government resources.
- **Government Bond**—a form of security sold by the government, which is often called a fixed income security because it earns a fixed amount of interest every year for the duration of the bond. Government bonds are issued to raise money for government operations.
- **Future Value**—the value of an asset at a specific future date.
- **Present Value**—the current value of a future sum of money or stream of payments, based on a specific rate of return.
- **National Debt**—the total amount of money that a country's government has borrowed.
- **Government Deficit**—a shortfall in a government's income compared with its spending over a given period of time, which then adds to the national debt.

End-of-chapter problems

1. Look up online what the Federal Reserve's Dual Mandate is and ex-plain why it is important for them to achieve these two goals.
2. Consider these questions about how the Fed operates:
   a. If Fed governors had terms of 3 years rather than 14, can you ex-plain why this could potentially lead to less sound monetary policy being conducted?
   b. Can you explain briefly the importance of having an independent central bank?
3. Suppose you win the lottery. You are given the choice of two different options: you can receive a one-time payment now of $1.5 million, or you can accept ten payments of $200,000, where you get the first payment now and the other nine each year over the next 9 years.
   a. Which of the two options do you prefer if the interest rate is 2%?
   b. Which of the two options do you prefer if the interest rate is 6%?

4. Your grandparents send you a check for your birthday in the amount of $500. Assuming the interest rate is 3%, what is the future value of the $500 in:

   a. Five years' time.
   b. Ten years' time.

5. Our discussion of future value incorporated interest rates but not inflation:

   a. If inflation rose from 0% to 2%, how would the future value of $100 in 10 years' time change, assuming an interest rate of 5%?
   b. How would you expect your calculation of present value to be affected by inflation rising from 0% to 2%?

6. Go to the U.S. Treasury's website or other online resources and find out what type of auctions are used to sell newly issued Treasuries to primary dealers, and then briefly describe the mechanics of the auction.

7. A 30-year bond pays an annual coupon payment of $250, has a face value of $1000, and the interest rate is 4%.

   a. Using a spreadsheet, calculate the price of this bond.
   b. Suppose the market is selling the bond described above for less than what you calculated in (a). Should you buy or sell this bond?

8. Some bonds pay zero dollars in coupon payments, and only make a face value payment in the terminal year of the bond. What would you expect the price of the bond would be relative to the face value?

4   The truth behind money creation

Objectives

1. To understand the basic functions of banks in the financial system.
2. This chapter studies the fractional reserve theory of money creation that is widely presented in academia, including in most money and banking textbooks.
3. Thereafter, we consider the credit creation theory of money which is how the real world really operates.

We all use the word 'money' frequently in everyday language, in phrases such as "they have a lot of money" or "that costs a lot of money," where we technically are not using the word correctly. In purely financial terms, the asset that is called 'money,' which fulfills the three functions outlined in the previous chapter, is critical for the functioning of the modern economy. Once upon a time, people traded goods and services in a barter system, whereby they carried out their business primarily within their local communities by trading goods and services for each other rather than using any medium of exchange. This requires a double 'coincidence of wants.' In other words, a baker who wants to buy a piece of furniture needs to find a carpenter who wants to buy a loaf of bread, and if not, no trade can be made. Money allows us to trade beyond our local economic circle by valuing goods and services in terms of a common unit of exchange. This expansion beyond our local community is further enabled by the commercial banking system, which enables us to carry out transactions all over the world. We can see evidence of the larger, global economy as we go about our daily lives. The internet places the ability to make purchases and transact business all over the world at our fingertips. Just imagine what our ancestors would think if they could see the way computers have revolutionized the business of banking!

For most of us, cash transactions are becoming more and more infrequent. This is true not just in the United States, but in countries all over the world, as the following diagram (Figure 4.1) displays (taken from Khiaonarong and Humphrey (2019), "Cash Use Across Countries and the Demand for Central Bank Digital Currency," *Journal of Payments Strategy & Systems*):

DOI: 10.4324/9781003251453-6

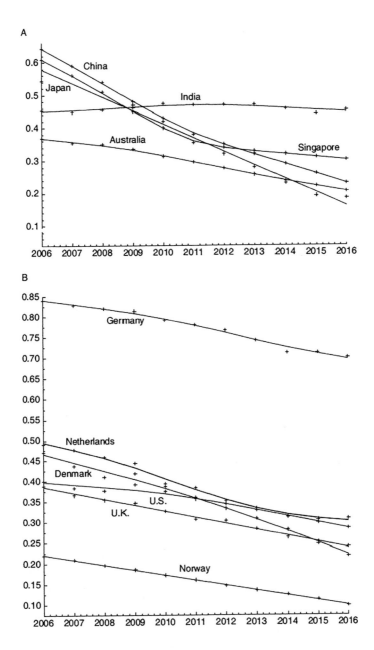

Figure 4.1 Share of Cash in Cash, Card, and E-Money Transaction Value, 2006–2016.

Source: Khiaonarong and Humphrey (2019)

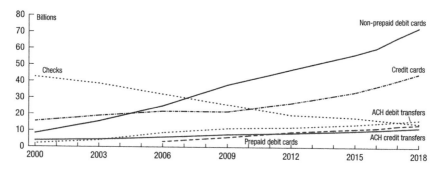

Figure 4.2 Forms of Payments in United States, 2000–2018.
Source: Federal Reserve

Some smaller retailers still trade primarily in cash but most businesses function by way of checks, bank drafts or wires. At the register, checks are being replaced by credit or debit cards that are linked to bank accounts and the ease with which we swipe our cards is a testament to how dependent we are on the banking system. Evidence of this can be seen in Figure 4.2 produced by the Federal Reserve (taken from the "2019 Federal Reserve Payments Study") where we see the use of checks plummet since 2000–2019, while the use of debit and credit cards has instead become the dominant means of payment.

But beyond the mechanics of a checking account, most of us do not really understand how the commercial banking system works. Gaining a basic understanding of the way the banking system operates can enlighten us to the mystery of money creation and the way it functions within our economy.

Bank regulation and oversight

With the economy operating on a global scale, oversight is needed to ensure that checks and balances are in place and stability is maintained. A financial crisis in a smaller country that has little international impact may be no more than a blip on the world's radar, but a banking system failure in a larger economy such as that of the United States, China, or the Eurozone could result in a crisis of large proportions. To prevent major banking disasters, all central banks in the largest nations in the world are members of the Bank for International Settlements. Commonly known as the BIS and based in Basel, Switzerland, it is called a *central bank for central bankers*. Formed in 1930, the BIS is the world's oldest banking and financial organization and its role as a stable advisor and resource in monetary and economic matters is well established.

Officials of the Federal Reserve and central banks of various countries convene regularly in Basel to discuss global coordination of monetary behavior, with an end goal of fostering an environment that encourages each country to be at relative equilibrium with other countries, thereby helping ensure that there will be proper credit supplied and available to the global economy. Over the last several decades, the Basel conventions have produced various rules and regulations which have been mutually accepted and implemented by most countries. Known primarily as the Tier I, Tier II, and Tier III Capital Ratios, these actions seek to provide a basis for measuring and regulating bank capital. Recall that capital is the difference between total assets and total liabilities and can also be thought of as the bank owners' equity. Simply put, they determine how much a commercial bank may lend relative to its capital base.

If a bank's portfolio of risk-weighted assets becomes too large and a significant portion of those loans defaulted, the loss from that default could wipe out the entire capital of the bank. This could put banks out of business and possibly threaten the banking solvency of a nation. By establishing ratios for measuring the amount of capital a bank must maintain on its balance sheet relative to the amount of loans it has outstanding, the BIS established a system of checks and balances that promotes global economic stability in an increasingly dynamic political and financial climate.

Bank reserve requirements

As we know, banks act as depositories who hold funds in safekeeping for customers either in savings or checking accounts. These accounts provide the means for individuals and businesses to pay bills and make purchases. Most of these transactions occur by way of checks or electronic funds transfers, i.e. internet banking, so cash does not physically change hands. It is simply a matter of making the proper accounting entries when funds are deducted from one account and transferred to another.

But suppose a customer needs to make a transaction in cash. He or she may walk into a bank and ask to withdraw funds from their account or simply drive up to an ATM machine and access their account from the computerized teller. If a bank maintained little or no cash on hand, there would be no funds available for the customer. So, there is a reserve requirement that directs the commercial banking system to maintain a certain percentage of deposits in cash. Generally, banks are required to maintain reserves that are roughly equivalent to 10% of total deposits, held in a combination of vault cash on hand and amounts on deposit at the Federal Reserve Bank.

While reserves were originally put in place to prevent a *run* on the banks, which would cause depositors to panic and withdraw their money and could collapse the banking system, the primary function of reserve requirements today, from a bank's perspective, is to ensure that there is ample cash available to support daily bank operations. And because they are in the business, banks know the level of reserves that they must maintain on hand. To ensure proper operations, they must maintain these levels without regard to the requirements being mandated by the Federal Reserve.

The business of banking

Now that we have an idea of the environment that banks operate within, we can move on to discuss the role that banks play in the money supply chain.

The modern commercial banking system serves three primary functions. First, banks act as depositories, accepting deposits from customers for safe-keeping and providing cash back to customers upon demand. This function dates back to a time when goldsmiths stored gold for customers. We no longer have a gold-based economy, but we still seek to deposit our money for safe-keeping and, hopefully, to earn a bit of interest while it rests in our account at the bank. Further, by keeping our funds in a bank account, we are able to easily transact for goods and services by writing checks, swiping cards or entering payment information into our computers. Banks act as the clearing-houses for all of these financial transactions, settling funds between accounts.

Second, and arguably most importantly, banks supply credit to custom-ers, lending funds to those seeking to borrow, and then profiting from the interest and fees associated with the loans. On the surface, this seems to be a matter of fact, basic service to customers. However, if we look a bit deeper, we come to realize that, by providing credit, commercial banks play a vital part in the creation and circulation of the money supply. In short, by creating credit, banks create spending power. And they do this with nothing more than accounting entries. While fairly simple, the concept is not widely understood, either in academia or by non-business individuals.

Third, banks help manage risk. If a layperson is in charge of making loans to potential start-up firms, they likely wouldn't have much expertise on which businesses are promising and which are not. The risk that stems from investment opportunities that we do not know much about is referred to as the *problem of asymmetric information* in macroeconomics. Namely, a new start-up firm will know more about their business (and the inherent risks) than potential investors do. Asymmetric information manifests itself in two ways.

First, *adverse selection* may occur. Suppose someone is willing to invest some money in a new start-up firm but has no idea how to tell which firms are good and which are bad. Since that investor does not know much about the firm, they choose to invest only in the cheaper options. Yet, the good firms need more investment and are likely to be costlier to finance. So, the choice of the cheap option will cause the good firms to leave the market entirely, and thus we are left only with the bad, risky ventures. Second, *moral hazard* could also occur, whereby a loan is given to an entrepreneur, but that entrepreneur doesn't use the funds wisely, and in fact, just wastes them away.

Even if we could overcome the problem of asymmetric information, the other issue is that we wouldn't have the time to do the necessary research if we have our own full-time jobs. But banks can do this research: they have the incentive to get it right, and the experts to do the job properly.

Two kinds of money

To understand how commercial banks create money, one must consider that there are actually two types of money. There is base money, which includes the physical currency that we are all familiar with, and bank reserves. To put some notation to this, the monetary base, B, is equal to:

$$B = C + R,$$

where C is currency in circulation and R is bank reserves.

Base money makes up a relatively small percentage of the total money supply. If you picture it as a pie, the wedge that represents base money would be surprisingly narrow considering that the mental image that comes to most of our minds when we hear the term money probably is a green banknote with a president's picture on it. This has been referred to as *outside money*, a term which is particularly applicable because of the fact that it is created under government authority (in the case of physical currency) or by the Federal Reserve (in the case of bank reserves), *outside* of the operation of the private sector.

The remainder, which is made up by what is referred to as bank money or *inside money*, termed as such because it is created *inside* the private sector, exists in the form of credit which is issued when banks make loans. Think about it as *electronic* funds; money that arises when an accounting entry is made to record a new loan. By issuing credit, a bank has given a customer new purchasing power. It is not cash and it does not increase the customer's net worth (because he also has a new liability to the bank), but it does provide the customer with the ability to spend. And, in a nutshell, this is how banks create money.

Fractional reserve banking and the money multiplier

We just defined what the monetary base is, yet the measure of money supply that is commonly referred to is known as *M1* in the United States. M1 includes the sum of currency in circulation and deposits held be banks. There is also an *M2* measure which includes savings and other small-time deposits (and retail money market mutual fund shares). We will use both measures of M1 and M2 in this book, but let's begin with using M1 as our measure of money supply. Hence, money supply, M is:

$$M = C + D,$$

where D is demand deposits held by commercial banks.

The process of fractional reserve banking describes how commercial banks, and not just the central bank, can in theory expand money supply. Here is how the story goes: Suppose we start with a world of no banks and there is $1,000 of cash in circulation in this economy, and it is held by one individual. This makes the monetary base equal to $1,000, which is also equal to the money supply. The next day a bank called the Old Gold and Black Bank opens for business. The individual with the cash decides to go to the OGB Bank and deposits $800 of their cash into a new checking account, which now becomes a deposit, while they retain $200 in cash.

The currency-to-deposit ratio, C/D, then becomes $200/$800 = 1/4. On the OGB Bank's balance sheet, the deposit represents $800 of liabilities, and is reflected as $800 in reserves on the asset side. The next day, OGB bank decides to make a loan. They determine to lend out $600 to another individual and maintain $200 in reserves. This gives them a reserve-to-deposit ratio, R/D, of $200/$800 = 1/4. The $600 cash is then given as a loan to the new borrower. Notice that the monetary base is $200 cash from the first individual, $600 cash from the second individual, and $200 in bank reserves, so it still totals $1,000. However, here is the key: money supply is the $800 cash from the two individuals plus deposits, which is the $800 in checking deposits from the first individual, so money supply grows from $1,000 to $1,600. Thus, the commercial bank has created money through the process of making loans from customers' deposits (see days 1 and 2 in the table below). And the process does not stop there, because individual two then makes a deposit using the C/D ratio again, and the bank has more reserves from which to make further loans (see days 3 and 4). The following table shows how the monetary base changes starting with no banks, then the OGB bank opens, and the process of two loans being made over four days is described (the loans themselves are bolded and underlined):

Changes to Monetary Base and Money Supply

	No Banks	Day 1	Day 2	Day 3	Day 4
C	1000	1000 − 800 = 200	200 + **600** = 800	200 + 120 = 320	320 + **360** = 680
R	0	800	800 − 600 = 200	200 + 480 = 680	680 − 360 = 320
D	0	800	800	800 + 480 = 1280	1280
B = C + R	1000	1000	1000	1000	1000
M = C + D	1000	1000	1600	1600	1960

Similarly, the following table shows what OGB Bank's balance sheet looks like to accompany the changes to the monetary base and money supply:

OGB Bank's Balance Sheet

	Assets	Liabilities
Day 1	R 800	D 800
Day 2	R 200	D 800
	L 600	
Day 3	R 200 + 480 = 680	D 800 + 480 = 1280
	L 600	
Day 4	R 680 − 360 = 320	D 1280
	L 600 + 360 = 960	

This process does not go on forever. You will notice that money supply starts to grow at a slower rate and would eventually fade away to zero. The ratio of the money supply to monetary base is:

$$M/B = (C + D)/(C + R)$$
$$= [(C/D) + 1]/[(C/D) + (R/D)]$$

If we call this fraction that combines the currency-to-deposit ratio and reserve-to-deposit ratio 'm,' we get:

$$M = mB$$

where 'm' is the famous *money multiplier* which, in theory, allows one to calculate exactly how much money has been created by banks (the final number for M in this example is $2500).

This theory of fractional reserve bank lending has been taught for decades in macroeconomics and finance. You will find it nearly in every textbook on this subject matter. It is elegant and neat, and academics think the math is quite cool! Unfortunately, the story of fractional reserve lending does not really match up to reality. Let us stress that this is a major point of departure of this textbook from almost any other description on money, banking, and financial markets. While fractional reserve lending is a neat theoretical description of money creation that is frequently promoted in textbooks and classrooms, it is *not* representative of the way banks actually operate money in the modern economy.

The truth about deposits and lending: where money comes from

According to the money multiplier story, a loan is created when a bank receives a deposit from a customer. However, banks do not lend money that is deposited by customers. Your cash that you deposit in the bank for safe-keeping does *not* become the basis of a new loan made to another customer. A bank does not have to have 'loanable funds' in order to make a new loan. Therefore, the notion that they must hold back a portion of such funds before lending the difference is simply false. In actuality, banks lend based purely on customer demand and qualified credit. Then, they seek to ensure that they meet reserve requirements after the fact. Therefore, deposits and reserves do not constrain banks' lending activities.

Let's look at how the mechanics of how the *credit creation theory* works in the modern banking system. If a customer who applies for a loan meets the bank's credit approval requirements, the bank will then extend credit to them. This is recorded on the bank's balance sheet with a debit to a loan receivable account and a credit to the customer's deposit account. This makes sense because the receivable from the customer is an asset of the bank and, since the bank has now effectively given the customer the right to demand the cash created by the loan, the customer has a new deposit account that is a liability of the bank. The loan led to the creation of the new deposit, not the other way around.

For example: Customer John Doe applies for a loan of $30,000 to purchase a new car. Bank A approves the loan. The bank's summary balance sheet just prior to making the loan looks like this:

	Debits	Credits
Assets		
Loans Receivable	$1,000,000	
Cash / Reserves	200,000	
Total Assets	$1,200,000	
Liabilities & Capital		
Customer Deposits		$1,050,000
Capital		150,000
Total Liab. & Capital		$1,200,000

When the loan is made, the transaction will be recorded with the following entry:

	Debit	Credit
Loan Receivable—John Doe	30,000	
Deposit Account—John Doe		30,000

Notice that no cash has changed hands. The bank did not need to have the funds on hand to loan to the customer. This is the 'bank money' referred to earlier. Now, the minimum reserve requirement is still in effect and the new deposit that was created when the loan was issued has now increased the bank's required reserves by 10% of the loan amount. For this reason, some refer to the new money that is created as 'fountain pen money.' If the bank does not have excess reserves already, it can either seek to meet its requirement by luring new deposit customers from other banks, often by paying competitive rates of interest on the deposits (leading to lots of marketing and advertising by banks in the real world), or by borrowing reserves from other banks who have excess reserves to lend. Either way, the lack of excess reserves at the outset did not limit the loans issued by the bank.

Because reserve requirements are determined based on an average of a bank's deposits over a set period of time, banks are able to carry on their day-to-day operations by lending first and then finding reserves later. In this example, reserves are adequate to meet the 10% requirement both before and after the loan is made. Let's take a look at the bank's summary balance sheet after the loan is made:

	Debits	Credits
Assets		
Loans Receivable	$1,030,000	
Cash / Reserves	200,000	
Total Assets	$1,230,000	
Liabilities & Capital		
Customer Deposits		$1,080,000
Capital		150,000
Total Liab. & Capital		$1,230,000

You can see that the only balances that changed were the loans receivable and the customer deposits. Cash and reserves did not change hands at all. Now, of course, if John Doe actually spends the loan funds by withdrawing cash, those funds will leave the bank and the total reserves on the bank's balance sheet would reflect that decrease in cash on hand. But that would happen regardless of the type of funds being withdrawn.

Similarly, if a customer writes a check from his checking account, funds are issued from the bank either in cash or by electronic entry. So, cash and reserve balances change continuously all day long without regard to any loans being made. Keep in mind, however, that when loan funds leave one bank to purchase a car, they end up being deposited in another bank, increasing that bank's reserve balance. So, if we view the banking system in the aggregate, as if it was one big bank with lots of branches, the total loans, deposits and reserves would be the same, with the funds just shifting among the branches. The funds will continue to circulate through the economy until the loan, whether in part or in full, is eventually paid back.

Since we know that adding to the money supply requires creation of a new asset, it follows that the money supply can only contract when an asset is destroyed. And since, when the borrower repays the lender, he is using an existing deposit to do so, an asset is being removed each time a payment is made. Therefore, the deposit that was created when the loan originated is correspondingly extinguished when the loan is paid back, completing the cycle of money creation.

Think about the credit creation theory in reality: we do not walk up to a teller's counter when we apply for a loan. Lending decisions are instead handled by a separate department. Every day, while loan decisions are being made, cash deposit and withdrawal transactions are continuously being processed. If a bank could only make a loan if reserves were held in adequate amounts, it would be a circular process, almost like a dog chasing its own tail to use an amusing analogy. Considering the number of branches operating for most regional banks, there would be no consistent way to determine cash on hand in a real time manner in order to either approve or deny a loan request. Loans are always made independent of reserve balances.

Of course, in practice, a bank's upper management would have a general idea of where the reserve balances were hovering. And there are different levels of approval required for loans over certain thresholds. But these management practices are in place to keep things running smoothly and efficiently, not as a function of reserve requirements. As is required by Federal regulations, the bank will ensure that it still meets the required reserve balances based on periodic historical measurements. So, there is a window of time for banks to go back and look at a certain specified period, usually around two weeks, to determine the bank's average total deposits. Then, an average of the cash and reserve balances for that period is calculated to determine if the bank is in compliance. But the key point is that this occurs after the bank loan has been issued, which contrasts with the prevailing view of money creation.

The credit creation theory of money that we have just outlined illustrates how individual banks create money without relying on their holdings of deposits. Not only do banks not lend deposits, they create new deposits as a result of their lending. Indeed, the Bank of England in some of its own published work has stated that the fractional reserve lending theory is a misconception, while the credit creation theory of money is the reality (McLeay, Radia, and Thomas (2014), "Money creation in the modern economy," Bank of England, *Quarterly Bulletin* 2014 Q1). There is also some scholarship in the academic literature that empirically verifies this claim using data, where the credit creation theory matches up to real-world banking behavior much better than other theories of money creation (such as Werner (2014), "Can Banks Individually Create Money Out of Nothing? – The Theories and the Empirical Evidence," *International Review of Financial Analysis*).

Additional restrictions on money creation

If banks can create fountain pen money out of thin air, then what is stopping them from just creating money indefinitely without any restriction? As the Bank of England explains in some of its research, there are three restrictions on the process of money creation even when using the credit creation theory of money. First, banks will limit themselves according to profits. In other words, loans will only be made if they are expected to lead to profits, and if they are not overly risky. Indeed, regulations are still in place to prevent overly risky loans. Second, the behavior of households and businesses will constrain money supply. In particular, the repayment of loans actually will reduce money supply in this theory of money creation. Third, monetary policy still ultimately constrains loan activity. For example, the central bank's target interest rate will influence the interest rate that banks can charge on their loans, which in turn will also affect how much households and firms will even want to borrow in the first place.

Role of the central bank

Picking up from the last point, let's see how the actions of the Fed can constrain what each bank does. Since we have established that banks do not lend their deposits and that loans are simply electronic funds created with accounting entries, it is clear that banks do not lend their reserves to customers. However, they do lend reserves to one another. If a bank has excess reserves on hand, as in the previous example, it can put that money to work earning interest by lending its excess reserves to a bank that needs reserves to meet its 10% requirement. This is not actually a loan in the context of extending new credit to increase purchasing power, as with a loan made to a bank customer. It is simply shifting reserves that are not needed to another bank who needs them and charging that bank for the right to use them. It is similar to charging rent for the use of an asset. In this case, one bank is *renting* reserves from another.

Who controls all of this? Recall that reserves are made up of cash on hand (vault cash) and balances in reserve accounts at the central bank. It is the Fed that is charged with management of the overall reserve pool by way of the interbank market. If one bank has excess reserves and another needs to borrow to meets its reserve requirements, the net result is a shift from the reserve account at the Fed held by the former to the reserve account of the latter. Again, no physical dollars actually change hands. It simply comes down to journal entries.

Bear in mind that all of this is reflected on the central bank's balance sheet where the deposit accounts are maintained. While each bank has its own balance sheet which shows its reserve account as a debit balance (because it is an asset of that bank), the central bank reflects the opposite side of each entry. Deposit accounts are liabilities of the entity holding the funds. If you have funds deposited at your bank, the bank owes that money to you when you ask for it. So, the reserves held on deposit at the Fed are liabilities of the central bank, because they are owed back to the individual banks who deposited them there. This therefore describes the third restraint on money creation under the credit creation theory as listed in the prior section.

Picture it this way: Assume the banking system is made up of three banks, A, B and C, plus a central bank (see Figure 4.3).

The total deposits shown on the central bank's balance sheet is obviously the sum of the reserves held by each individual bank in the commercial banking system. Each bank maintains its reserves on the assets side of its balance sheet. Conversely, that account shows up as a liability on the central bank's balance sheet. So, a look at the central bank's balance sheet reflects a liability for the aggregate amount of reserves in the commercial banking system.

Simply put, there is a pool of reserves that is spread around among the different banks. This pool is constantly circulating among banks. When one bank borrows from another bank, it simply shifts reserves from one to the other without disturbing the overall size of the pool. But that doesn't mean that the size of the pool never changes. Since we know that banks make loans based on credit and without regard to reserves, it is easy to imagine a scenario when the pool of reserves in total would fall short of the required reserves needed by the banks in aggregate. When this happens, the central bank steps in and increases the size of the reserve pool.

To understand how the central bank controls the pool of reserve funds, it helps us to understand the makeup of the central bank's balance sheet. Basically, the liabilities of the central bank are made up of (1) reserve accounts attributed to individual banks, (2) the government's deposit account, and (3) currency in circulation (because cash is a store of value that is backed by the government). Government bonds make up virtually all of the asset side of

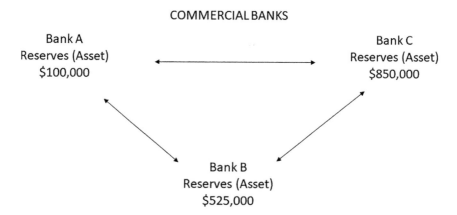

Figure 4.3   A Picture of the Banking System.

the balance sheet. And that is the key to the central bank's ability to adjust the size of the reserve pool.

How does it do this? Recall that in the United States, one of the duties of the Federal Reserve is management of the nation's money supply. The primary mechanism in the FOMC's toolkit is 'open market operations' which is the term given to the purchase and sale of Treasury securities by the central bank. Carried out by the Federal Open Market Committee (FOMC), open market operations can be used to either expand or contract the reserve pool in circulation. If more reserves are needed in the aggregate banking system, the FOMC simply authorizes purchases, through open market channels, of Treasury securities held by a commercial bank. Purchases are recorded by accounting entries which reflect deposits of newly created central bank money in the reserve accounts of the selling banks.

It is an asset swap of sorts, whereby the banks just exchange Treasury securities for newly created reserves. The bank's balance sheet changes in terms of asset makeup but its net worth remains the same. Of course, the banks are selling interest earning securities, but they receive new reserves in the process. And if they have sufficient capital and market demand is healthy, they will replace their securities with higher-earning commercial loans. The end result of the open market operations is that the banking system has a larger pool of reserves which will be shifted around as needed to meet aggregate reserve requirements.

Because the Fed is able to purchase the securities by way of accounting entries debiting the central bank's balance sheet to reflect the treasury security assets and crediting the commercial banks' reserve accounts, no money actually changes hands. The central bank just purchases the securities with newly created electronic 'money.' The Fed has the backing of the U.S. government, so it has the unique ability to create money out of thin air simply by way of a journal entry.

Conversely, if the Fed determines that the commercial banks' reserve pool is too large, it will sell treasury securities. All of this can be executed quickly, allowing the central bank to respond to changes in loan demand, as well as other factors that tell it when increases or decreases in the reserve pool are warranted. As we have established, reserves are a function of loans, not the other way around. And the central bank supplies reserves as needed to allow the banking system to meet aggregate reserve requirements.

Lending is capital constrained

We have already detailed that lending is constrained by whether the loans that banks intend to make will be profitable. Additionally, a bank's capital will curtail lending. Looking at a balance sheet, capital is the difference between total assets and liabilities. That is simple enough, but what does it mean? Think of a bank's capital as a type of cushion. If the bank was liquidated and all liabilities were satisfied, the capital is the amount of assets that would remain. Since it represents the amount of the bank's assets that would be there after liabilities were paid, it is the cushion available to protect it in the case of a decline in the value of the bank's assets.

But how does the capital relate to lending? Remember the Tier I, Tier II, and Tier III ratios issued by the BIS? Basically, a measure of a bank's capital relative to its outstanding loans, the capital ratio provides a risk-weighted measure that determines when a bank needs to slow down lending. Leverage ratios measure the bank's capital against its un-weighted total assets.

Clearly, banks make profit when they make loans to customers. Since they do not have to have deposits to lend and they can find reserves to meet prescribed requirements, banks could loan as long as there was demand for borrowing. With demand being a function of the market, a healthy economy and competitive lending rate environment could allow a bank to easily find itself with an abundance of customer demand. As long as the spread between interest rates on new loans sufficiently exceeds the rate that a bank would pay to borrow any reserves it might need, the bank stands to profit. Since banks' profits increase as their lending activities increase, it makes sense that they would lend every dollar possible.

However, if a bank has too much risk outstanding relative to its capital, it is jeopardizing its overall health and teetering toward possible insolvency. Moderate, balanced growth is the better alternative, allowing capital to grow along with profits, resulting in a gradual increase in loan portfolios. And, typically, that is what happens. Whether it is accumulating profits or the acquisition of investors that increases a bank's capital base, it provides a foundation for expansion of the bank's loan portfolio. Reserve levels do not come into play because the bank knows it can find any reserves needed to back up deposits created by extension of qualifying loans.

From a practical standpoint, loan officers are authorized by upper management to make loans up to a certain amount, with that ceiling being determined based on the bank's capital, granting them room to do business without being required to request specific permission to make each individual loan. So, assuming customer credit risk is being responsibly evaluated and managed, it is capital and leverage ratios, and not reserve requirements, that keep check on how rapidly a bank expands its loan portfolio.

As we close this chapter, let's remember that we have just made a departure from the story that is supported in academia, and moved toward the way money creation actually works in reality. For years, the economics profession has presented and argued in favor of the fractional reserve lending theory of money creation. While it makes for a nice numerical exercise—as we have presented in this chapter—if one deals with bank loans in the real world, this is not how it actually works. Instead, banks can create money by simply issuing deposits to their customers. So, in some sense, money is created out of thin air by banks, yet the system still contains appropriate checks and balances that limits the amount of money creation that banks are able to do. The Bank of England—the second oldest and one of the most widely respected central banks in the world—supports this very idea.

Key terms

- **Bank Regulation**—the laws and rules that govern the way that banks operate.
- **Bank Reserves**—the cash that banks have in their vaults, plus the balances in their accounts at the central bank.
- **Reserve Requirements**—the minimum amount of reserves that banks are required to hold.
- **Asymmetric Information**—the situation where two parties to a transaction have different pieces of information available to them.
- **Adverse Selection**—where two parties prior to a transaction observe different information about the quality of the product or service.
- **Moral Hazard**—after a transaction, one party to a transaction operates in a way that is counter to what the other party would desire.
- **Base Money**—the total amount of bank notes and coins. + Bank Reserves
- **Money Supply**—the sum of currency in circulation and bank deposits (under the 'M1' definition of money supply)
- **Fractional Reserve Banking**—the theory of how banks expand money supply by loaning out a portion of bank reserves.
- **Money Multiplier**—the number that describes how much money is created by banks assuming fractional reserve lending.
- **Credit Creation Theory of Money**—the theory that describes how banks can create money by simply issuing new loans that are not based on customer deposits.
- **Open Market Operations**—the process of the central bank expanding or contracting the reserve pool through the purchase and sale of government bonds.

End-of-chapter problems

1. Figure 4.2 presents some trends in the way we pay for goods and services over time:
   a. Do you anticipate these trends continuing in the future? Why or why not?
   b. What other possible forms of money do you think may be used for payment in the future?

2. This chapter mentions the concept of a bank run:
   a. Describe briefly what a bank run is and provide a historical example of this occurrence.
   b. What policies can prevent bank runs other than minimum reserve requirements?

3. The M1 measure of money supply includes currency in circulation, checking deposits, and also traveler's checks are still included.

a. Why are debit card transactions not included in M1?
b. Why are credit card transactions not included in M1?

4. Are the following examples of adverse selection or moral hazard? Explain your reasoning.

a. In the market for used cars, buyers cannot tell which cars are good quality or bad quality ones.
b. Someone with car insurance drives recklessly and doesn't lock the car when it is parked.

5. Suppose an individual is starting up their own new business, and they need funds for investment. They are considering doing this by issuing corporate bonds or by issuing shares of stock.

a. If the start-up issues corporate bonds with fixed coupon payments, will this reduce or increase the problem of asymmetric information?
b. If the individual was wealthy and did not need assistance in order to do the investment, is it still a good idea for them to issue corporate bonds or stock? Explain your answer.

6. Return to the numerical example of fractional reserve lending in this chapter, where we begin with $1,000 in cash and then the Old Gold and Black Bank opens. After two loans were made, money supply was at $1,960. Calculate the level of money supply after an additional loan is made.

7. Go back to the numerical example of fractional reserve lending again, and this time replicate the numbers of money creation when two loans are made, except savings accounts now exist. Assume that when people deposit funds into the bank, half goes into checking deposits, D, and half goes to savings deposits, S. The ratio of currency to total deposits, $C/(D + S)$, is 0.25, and the reserve-deposit ratio, R/D, is also 0.25.

8. Assuming the credit creation theory of money, an individual takes a loan of $250,000 from the bank in order to purchase a house:

a. Write down how the transaction is recorded on the bank's accounts.
b. Assume the bank had $2 million in loans and $500,000 in cash/reserves, with $1.5 million in customer deposits and $500,000 in capital prior to making the new loan. Write down the bank's summary balance sheet both before and after the loan is made.
c. Why did this loan not depend on the amount of deposits held by the bank?
d. How does the reserve requirement influence the amount of loans created by the bank?
e. Does this loan encourage the bank to seek more customers to make further deposits into their accounts or create new accounts? Why or why not?

9. Consider the credit creation theory of money:

    a. What is the main difference between this theory of money creation and that of fractional reserve lending?

    b. Explain the three reasons why money cannot be created indefinitely under the credit creation theory of money.

10. Suppose a bank has $10,000 in total assets with capital of $2,000.

    a. Calculate the leverage ratio.

    b. How much money does the bank owe?

    c. Is the bank solvent or insolvent if their assets fall to $8,000 in value?

5 Money, banking, and the real economy

Objectives

1. To understand how a central bank alters reserves to meet its target interest rate.
2. The term structure of interest rates is explained and examined.
3. The Quantity Theory of Money is introduced.
4. This chapter discusses how low and stable inflation is not necessarily a bad thing for the economy.
5. Quantitative Easing is described and discussed.
6. To understand how asset bubbles are formed.

We now have a firm definition of what 'money' really is, and we also have a good understanding of how commercial banks can create credit in the economy. To further our understanding of how the macroeconomy functions, we need to consider what happens when the money arrives into the banking system. As we know, central banks strive to achieve target employment levels and maintain mild inflation—depending on what their exact mandate is—but either way they adjust the money supply to achieve their objectives.

Recognizing that the creation of money is an accounting concept in that this money is created and moved around the system literally with accounting entries recorded in computers, it seems like a simple, matter of fact idea. In fact, the larger issue is not a question of, "How do I get the money into the system?" Rather, it is a matter of, "How much money does the system need?" How much is too much? How much is too little? Where is the healthy balance?

Benchmarks and targets

We have all heard that too much money creates inflation. The well-known saying, "There are too many dollars chasing too few goods," which implies that inflation is a function of the money supply, is simple, but relatively correct. The word *inflation* generally has a negative connotation, even inciting fear for some, especially if they lived through the 1970s. At the same time, we are led to believe that some inflation is good. It can be confusing. So how are

DOI: 10.4324/9781003251453-7

we to know what the right amount of inflation is? Historically, it has turned out to be true that 2%–3% inflation is a good thing, but more than that is unhealthy. In order to achieve this 2%–3% 'sweet spot,' central banks take the appropriate action to drive the economy in the correct direction.

We often hear that the central bank 'sets interest rates,' but that is not really the best description of what happens. In the United States, the Fed sets the Federal funds rate, which economists on the Federal Open Market Committee decide upon based on the environment in which the economy is operating at the current time. Commonly referred to as the *Fed funds rate*, this is the interest rate that lending institutions charge to borrow reserves from each other. Further, it is the benchmark rate upon which other lending is based, directly impacting other short-term interest rates as well as the prime rate, which is used by banks to build rates for longer-term borrowing.

But how does the Fed implement its target rate? It really is very simple. It uses open market operations to nudge the rate toward its target. The Fed looks at the volume of overnight lending between banks and from that it is able to get a read on the overall demand for reserves. If the reserve pool is too small, the demand from banks would push the interest rate up. If the pool is too large, rates would shift downward in response to decreased demand for borrowing. Since the central bank has an interest in maintaining a reserve pool balance that allows it to achieve its target interest rate, the Fed supplies reserves as necessary to meet the demands of the commercial banking system, which in turn pushes the Fed funds rate toward its target. Since we know that the central bank does not seek to restrict the amount of bank reserves supplied into the system, rather injecting reserves as needed to meet the aggregate demand necessary for banks to maintain the reserve requirements indicated by new deposits being created, it is clear that the Fed can use the demand in the reserve 'market' to control its benchmark rate.

Fortunately, a supply and demand diagram once again helps us to understand how the Fed can achieve their target for the federal funds rate. Bond traders at the New York Fed estimate the daily demand for reserves, while the Fed intervenes to manage the overall supply of reserves using open market operations. It is the job of the traders to engineer the supply of reserves in order to hit the Fed's target interest rate (Figure 5.1):

How are different interest rates related to each other?

We previously outlined that banks create money when they make loans based on the credit creation theory of money, and the primary factor that constrains the amount of money that banks can create is the interest rate that is set by the central bank. As we just discussed, in the United States the Fed targets the federal funds rate which is a very short-term interest rate. But what about all the other interest rates in the economy, such as the 3-month bond rate, the 10-year bond rate, and mortgage rates? While these rates are at different levels, they tend to follow the same pattern and move together (Figure 5.2):

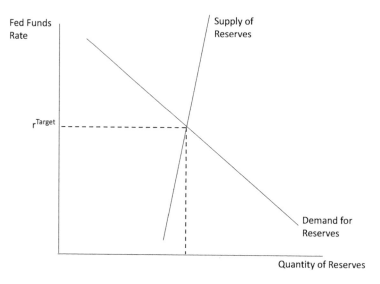

Figure 5.1 Supply and Demand of Federal Funds.

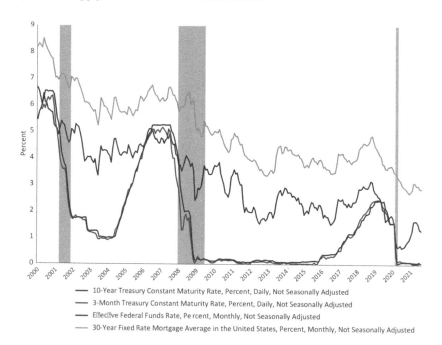

Figure 5.2 A Sample of Different Interest Rates.
Source: Board of Governors, FHLMC

The *term structure* of interest rates demonstrates how they are all linked. Suppose you are considering two Treasury bonds: a 2-year bond or two 1-year bonds, and you plan on saving for 2 years. Call the interest earned on the 2-year bond $R_2(Yr1)$, where the part in brackets states the time when the bond was issued. Interest is paid both at the end of year one and at the end of year two on this 2-year bond, giving you a total of $2R_2(Yr1)$ worth of interest. Alternatively, you could buy a 1-year bond in year one that gives you interest of $R_1(Yr1)$ and then buy another 1-year bond in the second year, giving interest of $R_1(Yr2)$.

For equilibrium to occur, the total earned on 1-year bonds must be the same as the total amount earned on 2-year bonds. If not, you would just buy one type of bond and not the other. Thus, equilibrium occurs where:

$$2R_2(Yr1) = R_1(Yr1) + R_1(Yr2)$$
$$R_2(Yr1) = 1/2[R_1(Yr1) + R_1(Yr2)]$$

It turns out that we could have applied the same logic to the choice between 1-year bonds and 3-year bonds:

$$R_3(Yr1) = 1/3[R_1(Yr1) + R_1(Yr2) + R_1(Yr3)]$$

So, the interest rate of the longer-term bond is the average of the interest rates on the 1-year bonds, which is the shorter-term bond. This now gives us a relationship between different interest rates. In general, the relationship will be:

$$R_N(Yr1) = 1/N[R_1(t) + R_1(t + 1) +...+ R_1(t + N-1)]$$

where N is the length in years of the bond, and t is the current year. To bring this equation closer to reality, we need to add two things. First, we don't really know what the future 1-year rates are going to be, so we should make it clear that those future rates are forecasted rates. We will do this by putting an 'E' in front of the term which stands for 'expected.' Finally, investors are really not indifferent between a 1-year bond and a 30-year bond if the expected rates are the same—they will also expect a term 'premium' for holding that bond for that amount of time, so we will add that in too:

$$R_N(Yr1) = 1/N[R_1(t) + ER_1(t + 1) +...+ER_1(t + N-1)]+ Premium_N$$

The above equation is the term structure of interest rates which shows how a short-term rate, such as the Fed funds rate, is related to longer-term rates. Typically, when the Fed adjusts the Fed funds rate, this then has a knock-on effect on other rates. We can even display this relationship graphically by plotting the 'yield curve' (Figure 5.3):

Usually yield curves are upward sloping. Often when they invert and start to slope downward, it is a sign that a recession or downturn may be impending.

Interest on reserves

In recent years, the Federal Reserve has implemented another measure to help control benchmark rates. Legislation passed by Congress in 2006

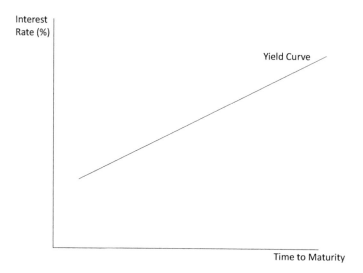

Figure 5.3 The Yield Curve.

authorized the Federal Reserve to begin paying interest to commercial banks on excess reserve balances. This was not a new idea. In fact, the idea has been around for decades. And, although the timing made it seem as if the *interest on reserves* notion was somehow related to the Quantitative Easing program rolled out in response to the recession, it actually was passed earlier with the intention of supplementing monetary policy by offering an additional way for the Federal Reserve to control the Federal funds rate.

By paying interest on reserves, the Fed is able to increase reserve balances without concern that it will push the Fed funds rate lower than targeted. Although the rate is minimal, by paying the banks some interest, the Fed is converting excess reserves into income producing assets for the banks. That tends to slow interbank lending activity, during circumstances when that is of concern, and it makes banks more amenable to maintaining excess reserve balances.

While the legislation was originally passed in 2006 and scheduled to be implemented in 2011, it was accelerated by the 2008 Emergency Economic Stabilization Act. This move proved to be particularly important for monetary policy, as the need to flood the banks with reserves in response to the banking crisis saw excess reserves at historic highs and pushed the Federal funds rate to historic lows. The interest rate on excess reserves effectively establishes a lower bound on the Federal funds rate, helping the Fed fine-tune its target.

Because the Federal funds rate serves as the base rate upon which other lending rates are built, the Fed can use it as a trigger point to help control the overall inflationary pressure in the economy and maintain a healthy equilibrium. When the Fed funds rate is low, interest rates on loans tend to decline, encouraging borrowing. This fuels the economy. So, if the Fed determines that stimulus is needed, it can inject reserves into the pool and drive the Fed funds rate down in an attempt to make consumers more interested in obtaining new credit.

The opposite effect happens if the Fed tightens reserve balances and allows the Fed funds rate to adjust upward. So, by influencing the overall demand for borrowing in the economy, the Fed can exert some control over the money supply and, thus, control inflationary pressure. The Federal Reserve Board understands that it is targeting a rate at which the system will achieve the ideal balance to encourage moderate inflation, but not so much that it will become overheated and allow inflation to grow unchecked. We can think of the Fed's ability to target a rate as both a brake and an accelerator on money supply creation.

More on inflation

Perhaps the most famous quote about inflation came from the late Milton Friedman, a much -respected economist at the University of Chicago, who stated that, "inflation is always and everywhere a monetary phenomenon" (from Friedman (1963), "Inflation: Causes and Consequences, Asia Publishing House"). Since inflation is understood to be a rise in the average prices of goods and services in the economy, that summation seems almost too basic. Of course, inflation is a monetary phenomenon! It is about money! But, just as different academics have argued over time as to what really causes inflation, misunderstandings persist even in our modern economy.

Friedman proposed the theory that inflation is all about the money supply. How much money is in the system? Too much money will create inflation, too little may cause deflation. As a monetarist, he believed that a restrictive money supply, too inadequate to feed the natural behavior of the economy, would cause prices to fall because too little money chasing too many goods would result in situation where supply exceeds demand. Conversely, if there is too much money in the economy, then prices will increase in response to demand which is outpacing supply.

Using the well-known *Quantity Theory of Money*, we can see the mathematical version of Friedman's ideas. The quantity theory equation states that $MV = PY$, where M is money supply, V is the velocity of money, P is the price level, and Y is real GDP. There is some evidence that the velocity of money—which measures how often a dollar bill circulates around in our economy over a given period of time—tends to be relatively stable, while real GDP is determined by factors such as capital, labor, and technology. If this is true, then from $MV = PY$, changes in M must filter through to changes in P, and a change in P is the very definition of inflation. When presented this way, this seems quite logical. However, this is a prime example of a theory that can be best explained with a clear understanding of the way that the modern monetary system actually works.

So, what actually causes inflation? This is a key economic question. After all, if we understand what triggers a certain event, then we can prescribe the best methods to prevent it from happening. Well, Friedman was partially correct. Inflation does in fact bear a relation to the size of the money supply in the economy. And while monetarists will argue that there is a causative effect, most economists who base their theories on the mechanics of the modern monetary system believe that increases in the money supply are more likely to be a reaction to inflationary pressures or, sometimes, a corollary occurrence with inflation but not actually the cause.

Think about the way the money supply is adjusted. While central bank intervention might increase the money in the reserve pool or alter the mix of assets in the economy through open market operations, the overall money supply only expands when new credit is created by the banking system. And the demand for credit would only stem from either a need to increase manufacturing output or perhaps a desire for investment or consumption. But the increase in demand would always be ahead of the extension of credit, therefore it is demand for new loans that leads to increases in the money supply. And, since we know that demand for credit is a function of confidence in the economy, we could actually say that confidence plays a much more critical role than the money supply when it comes to driving inflation. Economists who advocate for this view of inflation would point to a model called the *Phillips curve*, which shows that the change in demand and spending in the economy is the primary determinant of inflation, at least over the short run.

As the catalyst for loan demand, confidence is key when consumers make purchasing decisions. If a buyer fears that prices will soon increase, they may feel inclined to accelerate a purchasing decision. While it is fear of inflation that motivates that purchase, there must be confidence to support the choice to go ahead and borrow the funds they need. Similarly, if a consumer believes prices are stable, or even falling, a purchasing decision may be deferred. If they have concerns about their economic future, their confidence will falter, and they will not be motivated to take on new credit.

Does this mean that Friedman and all of the other monetarists were wrong? No, it simply means that they may have mischaracterized the interplay between credit creation and the money supply. Indeed, they are likely referring to a broader and longer time horizon than what we really base our decisions on in the real world. Like some other schools of economic thought, their ideas do not match up to the way the modern banking system works and its primary role in the creation of money. They may have missed the fact that, without demand for credit, the money supply simply cannot increase. And those misunderstandings may have fueled a belief that increases in the money supply could be forced. Still, there are lessons to be learned from those who have penned economic thoughts and theories through the years, not the least of which is the fact that a basic familiarity of accounting and banking is essential to understanding the way the economic world works.

So, if inflation is not a function of the money supply, but more a reaction to economic confidence and demand, then why are we led to believe that inflation is a bad thing? The mere mention of inflation in a headline causes immediate fear and concern, painting a picture of falling portfolios and rampant price increases. In truth, inflation is a bit like an out-of-town visitor, tolerable in small doses but wearing out its welcome if it hangs around too long. We do need a moderate bit of inflation because without it, the economy would suffer from stagnation. One can even demonstrate that some positive inflation is helpful in the labor market, as it allows businesses to adjust the real wage—wages once accounting for inflation—up or down depending on whether we are in a boom or a recession. A thriving economy will naturally evolve with a touch of inflation, which is a sign of increased productivity, as it moves forward. A healthy rate of inflation is evidentiary of an economy that is accomplishing more with fewer resources, thereby increasing GDP. But, of course, excessive inflation can cause uncertainty and a loss of confidence which may cause a pullback in investment and consumption, slowing GDP.

History proves that the ideal economic equilibrium with optimum GDP expansion requires an inflation rate of around 2%. When inflation hovers in that range, the economy has enough forward momentum to drive productivity yet keep prices in check, ensuring sound growth. And steady growth feeds right back into the level of confidence in the economy.

Something else that is worth saying is that the number of the inflation rate being at 2% is not entirely crucial in and of itself. The number could also be 3% or 4%. What is most crucial is that it stay stable at that rate. Why? This enables households, firms, and markets to make wise financial decisions with less uncertainty and greater confidence. Here's another way to see the problem. Suppose you are running short of cash and you need to buy a gift for a family member because it is their birthday, and you totally forgot to buy something. Your friend agrees to lend you $100, and you agree to give them $100 back in one week's time. In this simple example, you are the borrower and your friend is the lender.

Suppose over the course of the week that the prices of goods and services unexpectedly rise. When you give the $100 back next week, in *real terms*, which means the quantity of things that one can actually buy, you are returning less back to your friend. So, this higher-than-expected inflation was bad for the lender.

On the other hand, if prices fell during that week, you are paying back more in real terms than you borrowed when you hand over the $100. In this situation, the borrower is left worse off. So, if inflation is higher than expected, lenders are worse off. If lending slows down because of this, it could lead to an economic slowdown—such as happened in 2008–2009. If inflation is lower than expected, this is bad for borrowers, and if borrowers start spending less, this could also lead to a recession—there are numerous examples of this happening in the past. Thus, either way, the prospect of a recession looms as soon as inflation becomes volatile and unpredictable.

So, while experts such as Milton Friedman may propose that inflation is a function of the money supply, a clear understanding of the banking system leads us to take it a step further. Yes, changes in the money supply may be related to inflation. But they do not cause it. Prices are generally a function of supply and demand and inflation can happen regardless of changes in the amount of money in circulation. Increases in demand for certain categories of assets, such as oil or building supplies, may push up prices throughout the economy, as the Phillips curve says may happen. Changes in the availability of resources, such as fuel or agricultural produce, can affect the supply of goods, which may also result in price inflation. And, yes, increases in lending can drive prices up if the resulting increase in spending power is not balanced with growth in productive output. If costs and prices rise at uneven rates, potential business losses can create disruption and destabilization throughout the economy. Healthy economic growth is a balance of credit expansion and increasing output and GDP. Again, the key is balance and the catalyst is confidence. And if those elements are in place, there will be a natural rate of inflation which drives the productive engine of the economy.

Quantitative easing by the Fed

With the knowledge that the central bank will feed reserves into the system as required to meet demand, how can it ensure that the banking system as a whole does not continue lending beyond a point that is healthy for the economy? Is there a point at which the Fed would simply stop supplying reserves in the United States? From a practical standpoint, the answer is no. The Fed is motivated to supply reserves as needed in order keep the Fed funds rate at target. After all, the Fed's end goal is to maintain healthy inflation and employment levels.

That leads us to consider 'quantitative easing' or 'QE,' as it is often called. With the 2008–2009 recession still fresh in our minds and news reports, most of us are quite familiar with the term, which sounds very sophisticated and powerful. But, beyond a basic understanding that it has something to do with trying to help a sluggish economy, most people do not really understand what it means. Very simply, it is open market operations on a grand scale. Before such measures are undertaken, the Fed would have, through normal open market operations, targeted the Fed funds rate as low as it could feasibly go. If that has not sufficiently bolstered consumer confidence to encourage spending, QE could be initiated in an attempt to give the economy a nudge.

In order to provide liquidity for the banking system, the Fed initiates the purchase of Treasury securities in exchange for reserves. The mechanics are basically the same as the routine open market operations carried on by the central bank, with the distinction that, in QE, the securities being purchased may include longer-term treasuries, as well as mortgage-backed securities, municipals or other financial debt instruments and the amount of bonds being purchased is pre-determined with a specific time period for execution of the plan. In addition, QE involved buying assets from non-bank financial companies such as pension funds and insurance funds, which typical open market operations do not do. Basically, QE is an asset swap in which the Fed provides liquid reserves to banks in exchange for less-liquid securities. So, the Fed is pumping up bank reserves.

However, we know that simply feeding reserves into the system will not increase credit or trigger increases in loans. Only customer demand for borrowing will do that. If banks are not loosening credit standards, borrowing will remain stagnant. And if the economy is wrought with fear and uncertainty, indicative of a lack of consumer confidence, customer demand will not increase. From a consumer's standpoint, borrowing entails risk and a prudent person will not undertake new risk without confidence that there is an upside. Confidence inspires the courage to take on risk with an eye toward future growth. New borrowing translates to an increase in the money supply. Without this optimism, the banking system stagnates.

So, given the massive amount of reserves pumped into the system with QE1, QE2, and QE3, what is the purpose of QE? Most news reports maintain that stimulus money is intended to re-kindle GDP growth, energize the private sector to spend money, and push the economy forward. Some of the government bailout programs did serve to bolster the private sector. But the degree to which QE accomplishes those objectives is a point of debate and economists often disagree on the overall effectiveness of the program. While it is possible that certain categories of assets, such as real estate or bonds, could see a rise in values if the Fed purchases related securities in the open market, causing a slight increase in demand, the direct effect of QE is minimal. After all, the real end effect is that the balance of equities held by the banking system has been altered by virtue of swapping one asset (Treasury securities, mortgage-backed securities, etc.) for another (reserves) but the total of net equities held has not changed at all. And, without an increase in loan creation, the money supply has not been increased.

We can look to the 2008–2012 rollout of QE as an example. While there were variables, such as the fact that some of the equities purchased with QE1 were severely discounted (i.e. mortgage securities) as compared with QE2 or QE3, it is evident that the expected stimulus in terms of credit expansion did not happen. QE did help stabilize the banking system.

The economy was spiraling into recession and unemployment was on the rise. As real estate began to lose market value, the rate of borrower defaults began to increase. Banks' loan portfolios quickly lost value, throwing capital ratios off substantially. Faced with a drop in income as well, many banks were clearly in trouble. By pumping reserves into the system, QE propped up the banks by providing liquid assets (reserves) while at the same time sweeping their balance sheets clean of some of the subprime mortgages which were purchased by the Fed as part of QE1. To the extent that it stopped the trend, this helped hold bank insolvency (i.e. assets valued too low to cover liabilities and cash levels inadequate to meet demands) at bay.

As banks regained some stability, some of the public's confidence in the viability of the banking system was restored, but overall, the effect of QE on the economy was negligible. This is evident in the fact that QE1, although aimed at supporting the credit market, had little economic impact. Additional phases were subsequently rolled out as QE2 and QE3, both of which focused on purchasing Treasuries rather than mortgage-backed securities, and both of which simply added reserves into the banking system without much, if any, real economic impact, other than helping maintain low borrowing costs for the Treasury. Most of the reserves poured into the banking system have remained there as 'excess' reserves, meaning that banks' lending portfolios did not increase.

Some argue that it was all for naught, although keeping the reserves in place served to maintain stability in the banking system through a slow period of recovery. Lowered yields in the bond market did not push investors into riskier assets, as speculators expected. Thus, values were not revived, and optimism and growth remained sluggish. As for the factors behind the outcome of QE and its overall success as a matter of policy, the debate will continue and economists will surely have differing opinions. The one certainty is that we can learn from watching history unfold so as not to repeat our mistakes in the future.

More about interest on reserves

In good economic times, the interest paid on reserves is just part of the Fed's toolkit. In times of crisis, it provides the Fed with the ability to pour reserves into the system while still being able to maintain a floor on its target rate. During the 2008–2009 recession, the Fed, with its Quantitative Easing programs, made monumental attempts at stimulus. Yet, due to pervasive lack of economic confidence, loan demand did not materialize. Banks were in a holding pattern. With few new profitable loans being issued and their Treasury securities now sitting at the Fed, profit margins were being squeezed. So, the implementation of payment of interest on excess reserves, while intended to be an addition to the Fed's toolkit, served a secondary purpose of replacing some of the income banks had formerly received from their Treasury securities.

Whenever the Fed begins to taper QE actions, talk of unwinding its bond purchases invariably occurs. Some believe that it will lead to economic instability or inflation. Since we understand that, because loan creation and the money supply is not affected by the size of the banking system's reserve pool, we also understand that tapering QE will not lead to inflation. However, the markets may react to perceived changes in Fed policy and that may lead to instability. Therefore, the Fed must use caution and employ various tools to control the Fed funds rate as it alters its program. The interest paid on excess reserves allows the Fed to control the rate more accurately and quickly. Effectively serving as the lower boundary, the interest rate paid on reserves serves makes it easier to fine tune the rate, providing the ability to make adjustments without changing the levels of reserves.

Velocity and other economic indicators

Economists define the money supply in terms of layers which build successively upon each other, moving from the most liquid to the least. The most-narrow layer, called the *monetary base*, includes actual cash in circulation and reserve accounts at the central bank, while the broad category of *M3* encompasses larger, longer-term deposits, including institutional funds. *M2* includes all notes and coins in circulation, cash equivalents and cash accounts except for time deposits of $100,000 or more, so it is fairly representative of the currency available to us to carry out our daily activities. But why does keeping a measure of the money supply matter? Well, many economists believe that the size of our money supply can be used as one guide to understanding and predicting both short-term economic variables as well as longer-term movements such as inflation, helping Fed officials to determine the appropriate course of action in terms of monetary policy.

To view the money supply as an economic indicator, one must recognize that it should be expressed in terms of its relationship to other economic measures. For example, based on U.S. quarterly data from 1981 to 2019, M2 multiplied by approximately 1.8 equals the Gross Domestic Product (GDP), with GDP being defined as the total output of goods and services for, typically, a 1-year period. Figure 5.4 shows the behavior of the velocity of M2 over this same time period:

So, if M2 = $10,000,000,000,000 ($10 trillion), then GDP would be approximately ($18 trillion). That means each dollar is spent approximately 1.8 times in a given year, which means that *monetary velocity* is equal to 1.8. Since 1.8 is the typical velocity, if M2 or GDP change so that velocity drops to 1.4, it would mean that money is turning more slowly and producing less relative to GDP. This could signal an outbreak of inflation, because there is now surplus M2 in the economy relative to the norm. As the commonly repeated theory goes, if there is too much money chasing too few goods, the result could be price inflation or even an asset bubble.

Since a decrease in velocity just means that money is circulating relatively more slowly, it could also mean that there is a lot of money parked in bank accounts and not being used for consumption or to invest with, possibly because of a lack of confidence in the future or possibly a fear that the economy is over-regulated. It comes down to common sense. If there is a fixed supply of money and an economy is thriving, there are lots of economic transactions and money is changing hands more frequently. If economic

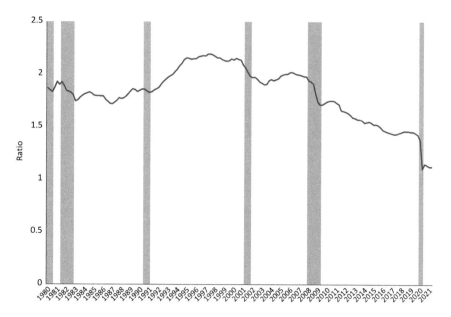

Figure 5.4 Velocity of M2 Money Stock in the United States.
Source: Federal Reserve Bank of St. Louis

activity cooled, or if there was an increase in the supply of money, each dollar would change hands less often.

So, it makes sense that velocity can serve as a gauge of the overall health of the economy because it generally is evidentiary of the rate at which the economy is growing. And while it can provide useful insight, it should always be examined along with other economic measures such as the size of the money supply, in order to provide the necessary context to make sense of the situation at hand. Where the size of the money supply can drive prices, velocity should be seen as a signal or a symptom of other economic conditions, but it does not bear a direct causal relationship to factors such as price inflation or asset bubbles.

This is not meant to be a statement about the proper amount of money supply or rate of velocity, because the definition of *proper* would be a moving target based on the economic, political, and social fundamentals in place at a given time. So, this should be viewed as simply an attempt to provide understanding of some effects of changes in the money supply and how the velocity of that money can impact the overall health of the economy.

Capacity utilization

Another measure of economic interest is *capacity utilization*. From an economic standpoint, capacity utilization is the extent to which production capacity is being employed. It is an indicator of efficiency in that it represents the amount of output actually being produced relative to the total output possible at a given cost of production. Figure 5.5 shows an index of capacity utilization for the United States, where it falls sharply during recessions (shaded areas) and it rises during periods of economic expansion:

Economists keep an eye on the capacity utilization rate, as it is often believed to be a predictor of inflation. It has been observed historically that approximately 82% capacity utilization will result in a low unemployment rate and relatively stable prices. Historical graphs and charts illustrate that at around 85%, that relationship no longer holds true, making an outbreak of inflation more likely if other economic variables are in place.

Notice the use of the word historical in relation to the 85% benchmark. While capacity utilization rate has long been a key economic indicator of interest to economists, its applicability has been questioned in recent years. In fact, data from the 1990s to the present seems to indicate that the relationship between the capacity utilization rate and inflation is much less stable than previously thought. Economists once believed that capacity utilization rates over the 85% mark signaled a greater likelihood of manufacturing bottlenecks and competition for resources which would lead to supply chain problems and place upward pressure on prices, hence the common use of the measure as a warning sign of inflation. Now, that predictive power is less clear.

Perhaps, it is due to the somewhat obvious fact that any measure of production capacity would be heavily weighted toward manufacturing industries, a segment that is shrinking in terms of importance to the American

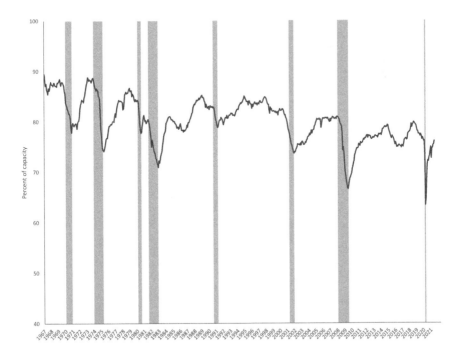

Figure 5.5 Capacity Utilization in the United States.
Source: Board of Governors of the Federal Reserve

economy. With the world becoming more globalized, much manufacturing has shifted overseas, and information and service industries have become more prominent in the United States. Information services need less capacity; therefore, technology and innovation can enhance GDP without a corresponding increase in capacity. While the importance of the capacity utilization rate in terms of predicting inflation in our modern economy may be unclear, the takeaway is that this measure of production capacity is one of many economic benchmarks available to those attempting to gain a better understanding of the way the economy works.

Unemployment and labor force participation

No discussion of basic economic indicators would be complete without inclusion of the unemployment rate. Figure 5.6 shows the United States unemployment rate which includes the uptick that was seen in 2020 following the onset of the Covid-19 health pandemic:

We can particularly observe how damaging unemployment is when there are recessions.

From an overall perspective, the rate of unemployment, defined as the percentage of the labor force that is actively seeking work, tends to be a lagging indicator of economic health. If the economy begins to dip toward recession, businesses tighten their belts and unemployment rises. As more businesses contract, or fail, more jobs disappear. The result of the job losses is like a domino effect, impacting both the public and private sectors of the

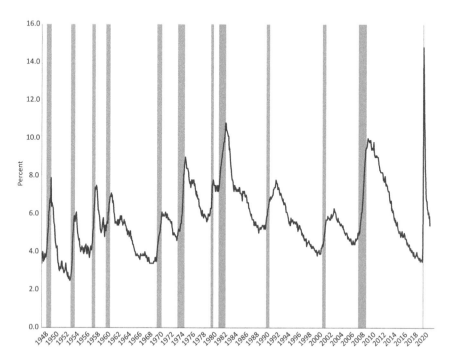

Figure 5.6 Unemployment Rate, United States.
Source: U.S. Bureau of Labor Statistics

economy. Individual incomes will drop, and fewer income and payroll tax dollars will be paid into the system. Lower incomes mean less spending, which affects local businesses as well as local governments, which rely on sales tax revenues to meet budgetary demands. When jobs are lost, fear and uncertainty infiltrate all areas of the economy, pushing confidence aside and painting a bleak picture of the future. As we know, confidence is an essential element without which an economy cannot thrive. And regardless of what other factors might be in place, if jobs are scarce, confidence will not prevail.

Clearly, the unemployment rate is a significant indicator of the current mindset in the job market. It is a mathematical measure of unrest in that it defines the percentage of the work force that cannot find employment. But it does not tell the whole story. What about the people who are not seeking work? Shouldn't a study of the productivity in an economy consider individuals who are able to work but, for whatever reason, choose not to pursue employment? The Labor Force Participation Rate is another employment statistic that the Bureau of Labor Standards monitors and publishes for the United States, and it is vital to use this alongside data on the unemployment rate (Figure 5.7):

Essentially, it is the measure of the percentage of the labor force that is currently working or actively seeking work. The pandemic of 2020 was particularly worrying from an economic standpoint in that the labor force participation rate fell sharply in a short period of time.

The labor force is typically defined as those between ages 16 and 64 who are physically and mentally able to work. By looking at the percentage of

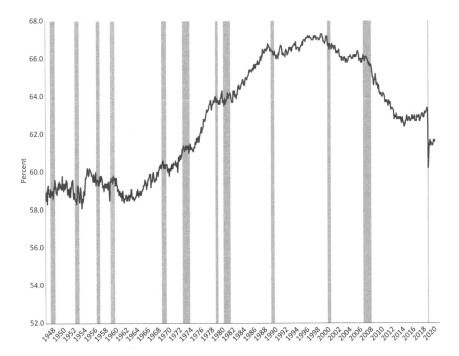

Figure 5.7 Labor Force Participation Rate, United States.
Source: U.S. Bureau of Labor Statistics

this pool that is either working or seeking work, thereby participating in the labor force, we can gain a different perspective on the overall health of an economy. There will always be individuals who choose not to seek employment, whether they are in school, raising children, finding satisfaction in volunteer endeavors or simply do not wish to work. And as the average age in a population changes, there will be gradual changes in the makeup of the labor force.

Changes in the labor force participation rate serve as signals to economists. If the rate decreases, it could mean there are sectors of the economy that have permanently contracted. Or perhaps more individuals have simply given up and are no longer trying to find work. By viewing the unemployment rate in tandem with the labor force participation rate, we can gain a better understanding of the condition of the employment sector and get a reading on the labor market, which, when combined with confidence, truly is the heartbeat of any economy.

Asset bubbles

We've discussed how price inflation can break out in the overall economy when the demand for goods exceeds supply. However, perhaps a more dangerous problem is that of asset inflation that is not the result of an excess of overall demand, rather excess dollars being funneled into a certain category of assets. Why? Because when prices for a particular asset, such as housing or gold, are continuously bid upward based on expectations of future growth, borrowers are able to borrow more and more on that artificially inflated collateral. Whether due to a flight to the perceived safety of a certain asset category, such as bonds, or investment opportunity, such as rental real estate, sudden spikes in demand for a particular asset category can result in quickly inflating prices. The artificially created values are unsustainable in the long-term and prices are bound to correct. At a certain point, borrowers cannot support the higher loan payments and the falling collateral values are insufficient to meet bank loan to value ratios, causing banks to call many of those loans.

This is exactly what happened in the 2008 housing crisis. Of course, riskier lending products such as subprime mortgages and the use of mortgage-backed securities to fund much of the expansion of housing-related debt compounded the problem. But at the core of the crisis was a build-up in housing values which was fueled by loose lending standards and low interest rates, allowing more and more borrowers to qualify for loans. The dream of home ownership became accessible for more people, but the quality of much of the new lending made for an unstable foundation. It wasn't a problem while the housing market was booming, but things changed quickly when the market corrected.

What led to the fallout? When a few houses in a neighborhood may be in distress or foreclosure at any given time, it will not affect the values of all the other homes. However, when too many houses are distressed at any one time, a *tipping point* is reached. Market values are determined largely by comparable sale prices. So, too many foreclosures or short sales will drop the average, resulting in lower market values for all of the remaining houses in the neighborhood. This may upset the required loan to collateral ratio of lending institutions who hold mortgages on the affected homes. Suddenly, loans are *under water*, meaning that the amounts owed on the properties exceed the values of the underlying collateral. Under pressure by regulators, lenders begin *calling* those loans, accelerating payment of the entire balance, even if the payments are current, possibly pushing more homes into foreclosure. As banks' income streams taper and balance sheet ratios become unhealthy, the systems *freeze up* and a widespread deflating spiral in value begins.

Real estate is just one asset category that can become overpriced. Think about stocks and bonds. When money is available at favorable rates and easily attainable credit standards, it can help to bring about speculation in investment markets. Think about it. When money is tight, people buckle down and stay the course. They may hold more cash and liquid assets. If money is available, they begin seeking alternatives. If borrowing is easy, or loose, and you are not worried about income, you will tend to put money in the place that offers the potential for the largest return. That means you will look to the asset category that seems to indicate rising values, often taking on more risk as you do so. If many participants in the market move into a particular category at the same time, demand may outweigh supply and prices will climb, creating a bubble.

Investment advisors know all about bubbles and may encourage you to invest in both stocks and bonds for diversification, and to weigh each according to expectations of growth in value of one category and avoiding loss in the other. This can be sound advice, especially if it entails spreading risk while also capitalizing on more rewarding sectors of the market. That being said, an investor should consider the economy as a whole before making any significant investment decisions. If there is a relatively large amount of money supply in the economy at a given time, bubbles may form, and diversification may not prevent massive losses.

For example, when there is more money circulating than currently needed to fund productive output, people will begin to look for opportunities. If that money begins pouring into the investment markets, both stocks and bonds may become overpriced simultaneously. If bubbles form and burst, market diversification will not prevent widespread fallout. And bubbles may form quite quickly. Potential investors may have money located in safe assets or other lower-yielding financial products. The owners of those assets, seeking a higher yield, may shift their money out of the low-yield products and purchase assets such as stocks and bonds. Once this shifting starts, stock and bond prices will be continually pushed upward as demand for the assets exceeds supply. As values inflate, the assets' fixed yields will reflect an ever-smaller percentage yield. Clearly, this cannot continue indefinitely, as an overpriced market will correct.

This scenario could occur in almost any market. Whether real estate, technology or even very specialized goods such as yachts, any market can develop bubbles if sudden demand drives values up. The stock market is particularly vulnerable, however, because it is fairly easy to enter, and the average investor may have difficulty monitoring factors such as supply and demand. So, what should one do to avoid being caught up in a bubble? Other than relying on advisors, stock market investors look to various economic ratios and statistical measures when evaluating stocks or bonds.

One such indicator is the Price-to-Earnings ratio. Historically, the U.S. Stock market has sold at a *P/E* or *price/earnings* ratio of around 15. That means that if earnings per share of a particular stock are, say $5.00, that stock may sell for a price of $75.00 (75/5 = 15). A P/E ratio of 15 also produces as 6.7% return (5/75). If that same share of stock is *pushed up* in the market to $100, the P/E rises to a dangerously high 20 (100/5 = 20), and the yield is pushed down to 5% (5/100 = 5). While this may happen in one stock without significant impact, inflated P/E ratios for an entire market segment could signal a maturing market or it could indicate the sudden formation of a bubble that may threaten an investor's entire portfolio.

A good story about an *overpriced* stock market based on an excess of available money comes from just before the great stock market crash of 1929. Joseph P. Kennedy, patriarch of the Kennedy clan, was having his shoes shined one morning on Wall Street. His shine boy began giving him stock tips. Kennedy listened thoughtfully, then, upon finishing his shoe shine, left the shoeshine stand. He called his stockbroker and basically said something along the lines of, "Sell all my stocks and hold the proceeds in cash!" Soon enough, the market crashed, and many investors lost everything.

Kennedy's reasoning was simple, and it applies to this very day. If even an unsophisticated investor was buying stocks, all others who would be investors were most likely already invested in the market. Any economic event of good news couldn't push stocks higher since there were no more buyers, yet any adverse or unexpected news could cause investors to begin selling, and doing so in an ever downward spiral, dropping values severely. When the market did indeed crash, Kennedy began buying distressed securities and other assets on his way to becoming one of the wealthiest men in America.

Looking forward

With so many opinions and conflicting reports circulating about the economy, it is no wonder that so many people find it confusing. Traditional relationships of the money supply to some of the often-used economic indicators have become skewed in recent years, leading some to question their applicability as tools. Indeed, many who are well-versed and educated in economics often have the story wrong. In trying to make sense of it all, the experts will track the multitude of economic indicators and attempt to predict what the economy is going to do next. But things change quickly, and it is difficult to hit a moving target.

Sometimes measures undertaken do not play out as expected. At the end of the day, it all really comes down to confidence. Many economists and others believe that when citizens, including employers, fear that fiscal policy and monetary policy are not conducted in a sensible manner and are not perceived to be *pro-growth* for the economy, those citizens simply lose confidence in the future.

The resulting fallout can be widespread, from decreases in spending to rising unemployment. Until confidence is regained, spending will remain sluggish. Rather than hire and invest in productive activities, which would entail much risk in times of uncertainty, business owners may tighten up their spending for fear of an uncertain future. When they are seeking *safer* alternatives for their money than growing their businesses, they tend to invest (speculate) in financial assets (stock, bonds, etc.). Of course, as there may be more and more buyers interested in certain asset classes, those assets' values are pushed higher and higher, giving rise to the belief that the wealthy are getting wealthier, even though it's really just rampant speculation driving the values upward.

These build-ups in value can be very fragile and the difficulty is to predict when they are going to peak and move out of some markets. Corrections can happen gradually, but it is more likely to happen with a short period of steep decline. A little hiccup may occur, causing buyers to panic and prices will plummet drastically. The speculative build-up in value is truly fragile and could burst at a moment's notice. That is why we use the very fitting term, *asset bubble*.

Key terms

- **Term Structure of Interest Rates**—the relationship between interest rates of different maturities.
- **Yield Curve**—a graphical representation of yields on bonds of similar type but different maturities.
- **Quantity Theory of Money**—a theory that shows that changes in money supply feed through to changes in prices.
- **Inflation**—the percentage change in aggregate prices from one time period to the next.
- **Phillips Curve**—a theory stating that inflation is negatively related to cyclical unemployment (or positively related to potential output less actual output).
- **Quantitative Easing**—a type of unconventional monetary policy whereby the central bank buys longer-term securities using open market operations in order to raise money supply and stimulate lending and investment.
- **Asset Bubble**—a dramatic surge in prices not in keeping with the asset's true underlying value.

End-of-chapter problems

1. Recent numbers reveal that inflation in the economy is higher than desired.

    a. What will the Fed likely do with their target interest rate in response to the high inflation?

    b. Should they buy bonds or sell bonds in order to achieve this federal funds rate target? Explain your answer using a supply and demand diagram.

2. Suppose it is 2020 and the 1-year interest rate is 5% and the 10-year interest rate is 8%. Draw a graph showing the likely path of the 1-year rate from 2020 to 2029. Use the term structure of interest rates theory to answer this question.

3. A bank issues a mortgage to a customer who is buying a home. It is a 30-year mortgage with a fixed interest rate of 6%.

    a. If the bank forecasts an average inflation rate of 2% over the next 30 years, what is their anticipated real return? (Hint: 'real' means adjusting for inflation).

    b. If it turns out that inflation over that 30-year period was actually 8%, who benefits from this and who is hurt between the bank and the mortgage customer?

4. Write down the Quantity Theory of Money Equation.

    a. If the velocity of money and real GDP are stable over time, what is the relationship between money supply and prices?

    b. If velocity is declining while money supply is increased, what happens to inflation?

5. Go to the Federal Reserve website and obtain post-WWII data on M1 and CPI prices for the United States.

    a. Draw a scatterplot of the data at the monthly frequency. Does the Quantity Theory story appear to be true?

    b. Re-do part (a), but now using 10-year averages instead of the monthly frequency. Is the Quantity Theory more or less apparent now in this version of the scatterplot?

6. The Phillips Curve states that inflation depends on the amount of demand in the economy:

    a. If aggregate demand falls during a recession, what can we expect to happen to inflation?

    b. If a supply shock occurred which raises firms' cost of production, such as a rise in energy prices, what can we expect to happen to inflation?

7. Consider Quantitative Easing:

   a. Why are short-term interest rates close to zero before QE is enacted?

   b. Explain in your own words whether the rounds of QE conducted by the Federal Reserve in the last 10–15 years have been successful at stimulating the economy.

8. Go to the Federal Reserve website and find data for 2020 and 2021's M2 and GDP for the United States:

   a. What is the ratio of M2 to GDP in each of these years? What explains how it changed from the number presented in this chapter?

   b. According to this chapter, does the change in this ratio predict more or less future inflation in the years after 2021?

6   Global monetary linkage

Objectives

1. To understand how exchange rates are determined and what the foreign exchange market is.
2. To analyze how and why currency trading occurs.
3. Different types of currency contracts are defined and briefly discussed.
4. To examine the Eurozone, how it operates, and what its relative advantages and disadvantages are.

Let's begin this chapter with a primer on currency trading. Suppose a U.S. citizen wants to purchase something from a seller in Germany and have it shipped to their home in the United States. Let's say the U.S. citizen wants to buy a German-manufactured piece of clothing (suppose it's a suit) that is only sold and produced in Germany. Whether the buyer purchases the item directly from the seller or buys it through a U.S. importer, let's assume that the seller will expect to be paid in euros, the currency of the Eurozone, of which Germany is a member. In order to complete the purchase, the buyer (or the importer) would need to exchange U.S. dollars for the equivalent number of euros. For instance, if the suit retails for €100, and the dollar-to-euro exchange rate was $1 to €0.85, then the U.S. citizen needs 100/0.85 = $118 which they will use to convert into euros, and then be able to buy the suit.

To do so, they could utilize the services of a bank, which would have access to the currency market through Forex. By the way—if you ever look up exchange rates online or in the newspaper—those exchange rates are those that are available to banks who are trading more than $1 million worth of currency at a time, and are not the rates available to the average person. Forex, which means foreign exchange market, is a worldwide decentralized market for the trading of currencies. Through Forex, the buyer could simply exchange into euros the number of dollars needed for the transaction, for a small transaction fee, of course. And that is a typical transaction that happens around the world billions of times per day.

DOI: 10.4324/9781003251453-8

Exchange rates

The mechanics of currency exchange are really quite simple. In our example, the American buyer of the German goods exchanges dollars for euros in order to transact business with the German seller. Now, in our digital age, we can purchase goods from overseas just by logging into a computer or even a smartphone. So, we may not actually have to go through the process of physical currency exchange. Still, whether we actually go to a bank or we use digital bank transactions to buy goods, the process is essentially the same. We are using our domestic currency, dollars, to purchase an equivalent amount of foreign currency. Even if you use a credit card to buy a foreign good, the credit card company is still performing some sort of currency exchange. It is a swap, based on the prevailing market exchange rates at the time we execute the transaction. It is quite simple yet can be very daunting for those who do not understand how the foreign exchange market works.

The spot market

The larger and more important point is not how the exchange is made, but rather, who or what controls the exchange rates of these many different currencies. Well, the market does, of course. But how does the market know which currencies, on any given day, are worth a little more or a little less than they were yesterday, relative to another currency? It comes down to supply and demand, which is a function of current economic factors, political activity, and general confidence in one currency's potential for future performance relative to another. Uncertainty or instability may upset economic confidence, resulting in suppressed demand and falling values. So, the currency market is typical of others, where the many influencing factors converge to result in an exchange known as a *spot deal*.

To understand how the *spot* market works in terms of determining value for a particular currency, let's consider a simple scenario using the U.S. dollar. To set the stage for our example, let's back up a bit and look at the economic big picture of the United States. Let's say that for this year, the annual GDP (by the U.S. Department of Commerce) is projected to be around 21 trillion dollars. With a few keystrokes, we can quickly access internet data that tells us that the average amount of money supply (M2) was about 15 trillion dollars in the same year. Remember that M2 is simply cash in circulation plus the amount of money that has been loaned into the economy by the commercial banking system and is now spread out into millions of bank accounts owned by you, me, businesses, etc. Those accounts are on the banks' books as deposit liabilities (remember, they are a credit on the bank's balance sheets because the bank owes them to the account holder upon demand). So, we have:

$$\frac{\$\,15\ \text{trillion M2}}{\$\,21\ \text{trillion GDP}} = 71\%$$

We awaken the next morning, search the web while drinking our coffee, and see exciting news! The headlines of two newspapers with worldwide circulation, The Wall Street Journal and The New York Times, exclaim:

CANCER CURED! AMERICAN COMPANY TO MAKE NEW DRUGS AVAILABLE IMMEDIATELY!

And a second headline:

NEW OIL EXTRACTION TECHNIQUES DISCOVERED BY TEXAS INNOVATORS: GAS PRICES TO DROP TO 75 CENTS PER GALLON IN THREE MONTHS!!

Wow! Obviously, this example is extreme, but the immediate reaction of all the world economists, currency traders, and everybody else who reads and cares, is to expect an unbelievably great upcoming year. They may envision something like this: GDP of 30 Trillion Dollars!

With the $15 trillion outstanding money supply (M2) to be circulated within a 30 trillion GDP, the ratio changes to:

$$\frac{\$\ 15\ \text{trillion M2}}{\$\ 30\ \text{trillion GDP}} = 50\%$$

The result, it would initially seem, is that each dollar circulating in this economy can buy more goods and services. Obviously, and immediately, each dollar becomes worth more, assuming that all else remains unchanged. But the reality is that each dollar becomes worth more very quickly as foreign investors buy dollars with which to invest in U.S. assets (stocks, real estate, etc.) expecting to profitably benefit from this rapid growth. But, of course, domestically, intense loan demand by consumers and investors would increase our M2 over time, restoring the M2 to GDP ratio.

Is this beneficial for the United States? Besides the obvious positive impact of such news, it makes each of our dollars able to buy more euros, or other currencies, so, now if we want to purchase something from Germany, it will cost fewer dollars to buy that item. The technical term we would use is *appreciation*, where the dollar has appreciated in value with respect to the euro. On the other hand, *deprecation* is the word we would use if the dollar lost value against a foreign currency.

Other factors could affect the dollar in a different way. For example, if GDP appeared to be continuing on the same path as before, and assuming that everything else remained the same, the trading value (exchange rate) of the dollar could remain the same. Or, it could strengthen for a different reason than rapid growth, such as a policy change.

For example, if the Fed decided, using its best wisdom, that too much money was in the economy, it could tighten its monetary policy, removing excess reserves through open-market operations, selling from its portfolio of Treasuries (assets on the Fed's balance sheet) to various commercial banks. This would be nothing more than an asset swap, which would not change the overall values on bank balance sheets, but it would remove liquidity from the banking system's reserve pool, putting upward pressure on interest rates, thereby discouraging some lending. The slow-down in lending, combined with the reduction in deposits resulting as loans were paid off, would decrease the amount of money circulating through the commercial banking system, thereby reducing overall money supply in the economy. Of course, with fewer dollars in circulation, the value of each dollar would begin to rise.

So, while some factors may be unexpected or unplanned, policy makers do sometimes have a hand in the amount of money in the economy. And, although Fed actions may not be specifically aimed at controlling the value of the dollar, the impact is sometimes a by-product of monetary policy changes.

With just a few examples, it is easy to see how many factors come into play each day that affect currency values. Of course, overall economic outlook plays a major role, as does political stability, both at home and abroad. Really, it all comes down to confidence in the future. Good and bad news throughout the world, the behavior of various countries' central banks, as well as lending behavior by the commercial banks, all send signals to the currency markets on a continuous basis. And with real-time reporting and reactions to such events, constant world currency revaluation should come as no surprise.

A simple model of the exchange rate

Let us paint a simple model of the exchange rate. Suppose you have $10,000 that you wish to save, and you are deciding whether you should buy $10,000 worth of U.S. Treasury bonds or $10,000 worth of British government bonds which you intend to hold for 1 year. What is the expected return on the U.S. bond? It is just the interest rate you will earn, call it R_{US}. What about the expected return on the British government bond? Well, here are the steps you would need to take: you first swap your dollars for pounds and then buy British government bonds. At the end of the year you earn the British interest rate on those bonds, and at that point you sell your British bonds for pounds and then swap those pounds back into dollars. Now, here is the tricky part: when you are calculating the expected foreign return in this example, we know the British interest rate, and we know the current dollar-pound exchange rate. But we also need a forecast of the dollar-pound exchange rate for 1 year's time, because that will be the relevant exchange rate for when we swap our pound earnings back into our home currency.

Fortunately, we can write down a formula that encapsulates all of these steps succinctly—the expected foreign return, denominated in the domestic currency, is given by the expression $R_{UK} + (X^e - X)/X$, where R_{UK} is the British interest rate, X is the current dollar-pound exchange rate, and X^e is the forecasted future dollar-pound exchange rate. In equilibrium, investors will be indifferent between dollars and pounds when the expected returns on the two are equal to each other:

$$R_{US} = R_{UK} + (X^e - X)/X$$

This equation is referred to as the (uncovered) interest parity condition, and the value of X that solves this equation is the equilibrium exchange rate.

The really useful part of this equation is that we can turn it into graphical form. Let's draw a diagram (Figure 6.1) that shows the expected return of the domestic bond (left-hand side of the interest parity condition) against the expected foreign return of the foreign bond (right-hand side of the interest parity condition):

The exchange rate that prevails in the market is X_1, where both curves intersect. Now that we have established this diagram, we can use it to show what happens if central banks enact monetary policy. If the Fed decides to raise interest rates, this shifts the domestic expected return curve to the right (see Figure 6.2), and causes appreciation of the dollar (X going down represents appreciation, and X going up represents depreciation):

Alternatively, if the Bank of England decided to raise their interest rate, then we would see the foreign expected return curve shift upward, which causes the dollar to depreciate (Figure 6.3):

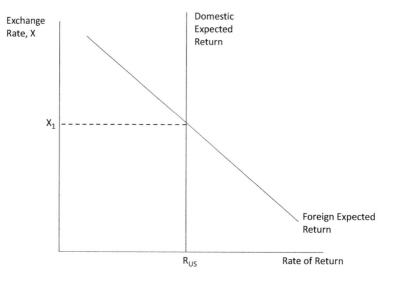

Figure 6.1 The Foreign Exchange Market.

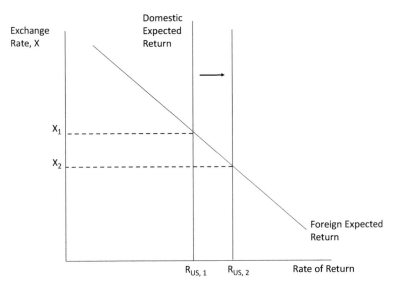

Figure 6.2 Increase in Domestic Interest Rate Effect on Exchange Rate.

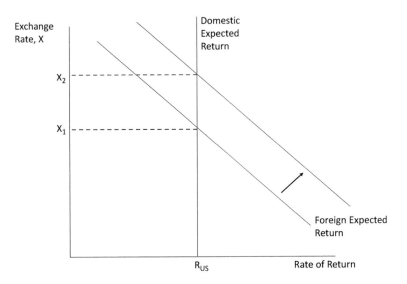

Figure 6.3 Increase in Foreign Interest Rate Effect on Exchange Rate.

Notice that if X^e went up, we would get the same diagram as in Figure 6.3. What goes into X^e, the forecast of the future exchange rate? Probably dozens, if not, hundreds of factors go into it: the state of the domestic and foreign economies, financial markets, industries, and governments. Confidence drives all of these things, so any shift in confidence between the domestic and foreign countries will cause a change in future expected exchange rate, which actually causes the current spot exchange rate to move.

Purchasing power parity

Economists and currency traders, as well as participants in international markets, keep abreast of certain market indicators in order to predict movement in foreign exchange rates. One such indicator is the measure of Purchasing Power Parity (PPP). Really a theory, it is the suggestion that exchange rates between currencies tend to push toward equilibrium, meaning that a basket of goods valued in one currency should cost the same in another currency, after adjustment for currency exchange.

What does this mean? For simplicity, imagine that a pizza pan costs $100 dollars in the United States. What would that same pizza pan cost in Mexico? Well, if the prevailing exchange rate indicates that one dollar is equivalent to 12 pesos, then you would expect the pan to cost 1,200 pesos, right? The formula that follows this is:

$$X = P_{US}/P_{M}$$

where X is the dollar-peso exchange rate, and P_{US} and P_{M} are the price levels in the United States and Mexico, respectively. What if you find out that Mexican companies are selling identical pizza pans for 800 pesos? If you own a chain of pizza parlors, wouldn't you be motivated to purchase the pans from Mexico? Assuming the products are equivalent, and shipping costs are not an issue, then of course you would take advantage of the savings opportunity. And if that is the case, then purchasing power between the dollar and peso is not at parity.

While it may seem like a great opportunity for someone who is in the market for pizza pans, we must consider the long-term effects of disequilibrium. Demand for pizza pans sold by U.S. companies would drop as those sales shift to Mexican companies, therefore the demand for pesos would increase. This would place upward pressure on the value of the peso relative to other currencies. The increase in demand would push prices for Mexican pizza pans up. At the same time, to compete with Mexican companies, American companies would have to begin reducing prices for pizza pans in an attempt to attract customers. As the prices for the pizza pans move up in Mexico and down in the United States, they will eventually reach equilibrium. This type of trading that has moved the market back into equilibrium where prices are equalized across economies is known as *arbitrage*.

The values of the currencies react to the changes and adjust as well, ultimately moving toward a natural state of parity. And while the overall market will not adjust due to the movement in prices for pizza pans, this same phenomenon is taking place across all markets all the time. Further, if the purchaser is not one retailer or a regional restaurant chain, but a giant like Walmart, then the stakes are suddenly much higher, and the impact is greater. Cost savings become much more meaningful at that level and business decisions will be motivated by those savings opportunities. It is yet another example of how human nature comes into play in our economic lives.

Markets shift and business respond, capitalizing on savings where they can while looking for the next opportunity. The common truth is that, absent intervention, markets eventually move toward equilibrium, proving the theory of purchasing power parity. And this is the point that those market watchers understand. They watch for changes in certain market segments and then use that information to make predictions about upcoming trends in the currency markets.

While the theory of PPP makes a lot of intuitive sense, the data reveal that it often does not hold. Why is that? There are numerous reasons, such as high transport or shipping costs, taxes, or trade barriers that nullify any potential arbitrage opportunities. Additionally, firms that have market power, such as through strong brands, may be able to price the same good differently in alternative markets if the demand for the same product differs across borders. Research from economists has also shown that testing whether PPP even holds is in and of itself a difficult and non-trivial exercise (for example see Zucman (2004), "The Purchasing Power Parity Debate," *Journal of Economic Perspectives*). Most economists conclude that PPP may not be useful at predicting the specific spot exchange rate at any given moment of time but can provide a useful longer-term benchmark of where the true value of a currency should lie.

Trading for profit

As in our example, the currency trading market evolved in accommodation of a necessary step in the process of transacting business with another country. It was nothing more than a means to an end. These days, when we read or hear about the foreign exchange market, we are most likely talking about something completely different. As with most other business and profit-making ventures, currency trading originated from a combination of opportunity and innovation. Made possible by our modern banking and communication systems, foreign exchange trading has grown into what is now one of the fastest growing investment market segments.

The basics of currency trading are fairly straightforward. It is a business model that, like other trading and derivatives market, has elements that resemble gambling. A trader is playing upon the constant fluctuation of currencies relative to one another, speculating that a particular currency will rise or fall in value. While it seems as if that should be a fairly simple bet, the underlying complexities of currency valuation make it a venture fraught with risk.

The industry is open to anyone, experienced investment managers and individual investors alike. And, with low regulations and no central market in control, entering into the world of currency trading is fairly easy. However, whether due to intimidation or lack of understanding of the way foreign exchange works, many smaller investors are hesitant to enter the currency trading arena. Most profit seeking trades are made by larger banks, investment managers, or hedge funds, as those are the market participants with the most experience and access to the most reliable information. And while the market exists to serve a specific business purpose, there is much speculative money to be made for those who truly understand the game.

While most individual investors will not ever participate in currency trading for profit, it is helpful to have some general knowledge about the way it works and the impact that it can have on general economic conditions. There is no magic recipe. Basically, currency trades are executed in pairs, where the investor is simultaneously buying one currency and selling another. It is an asset swap, just using one currency to purchase another. The opportunity for profit comes in when the trader speculates correctly and uses a currency that may be falling in value to purchase one whose value is rising.

Obviously, when the currency received in the exchange appreciates, the trader profits. For instance, suppose you exchange $100 for Japanese Yen at 10am one day, and you receive ¥10,000. The exchange rate was therefore $1 to ¥100 when you made the trade. Then, at 11am on the same day, the market moves, and the exchange rate becomes $1 to ¥90. When you exchange the ¥10,000 back into U.S. dollars at the new exchange rate you are left with $111, and have thus made a nice, easy profit. If a trader does this consistently, he can build up quite a nice number in his *gain* column. And for those larger and more experienced traders, leverage comes into play, raising the profit potential on the winning trades but also ramping up the risk for losses. And losses do indeed happen, with less than half of Forex trades being reported as profitable.

These currency trades, commonly referred to as currency swaps, are usually accomplished through contractual agreements between parties who deposit funds to secure the trade on the currency as values swing in either direction. At the time the contract expires, or is unwound, the parties settle, one with gain and the other with a corresponding loss. There are numerous, sophisticated types of these contracts used by professionals to execute these trades. These contracts are known as derivatives, as they are derived from the underlying asset—currency in this case—rather than the trading of the actual assets themselves.

So, who are the players? Well, the largest segment of the market, in terms of trading volume, is made up of banks. While banks of all sizes participate in the market in order to meet needs of customers who are transacting business in other currencies, some also enter into the market for profit. Those with investment departments may be executing trades on behalf of clients, with a spread on the trade that represents the bank's profit. And it is logical that larger banks, who hold substantial foreign currency in reserve anyway, would enter into the market in pursuit of gain. By using the reserves, which would otherwise be non-income producing assets, to play the currency trading game, they have the potential to use the bank's own capital to bring in profits.

Since we know that exchange rates are a function of values as determined based on supply and demand, the larger size of the trades being carried out by larger banks often has a significant effect on the values in the currency exchange market. With no central market in place, trades are essentially just bids and offers being made between traders. A large bank can sway the price of a currency just by making a successful bid which will alter the value of that currency. While it may sway values only slightly, this still adds an additional element of risk to the guessing game.

Large traders place their bets based not only on their knowledge of expected government actions, anticipated central bank moves, political activities, and the like but also by predicting what their fellow traders will likely be doing. And while profit seeking trades by institutional participants garner the most attention, a substantial amount of the activity in the exchange market is initiated by central banks and governments. Open-market operations, typically aimed at affecting interest rates, often involve foreign exchange activity (a central bank may purchase or sell foreign currency reserves out of or into its commercial banking system to alter the size of the pool of currencies relative to each other, altering supply and demand). So, government policies can drive the market in unpredictable directions, adding risk to the game for those who are in the market hoping to beat the average returns.

While most of us will not become currency day traders, we should be aware of the impact that those who do participate in the exchange market may have on currency values. Even the value of our dollar can be affected by these trades. So, while supply and demand for currency is the primary driver of value, the underlying factors that determine that supply and demand must be considered. Governmental actions and the like are certainly critical. But we must also be mindful that movement in the currency investment market pushes values as well.

Trading for currency movement protection

Of course, while some enjoy trading for speculative profit, the majority of currency trading is executed by businesses attempting to avoid loss from an excessive negative currency movement, the degree of which may be unknown at any given time. They will hedge their perceived risk. Let's use a simple example: two domestic companies, one an importer and the other an exporter, may have opposite interests in the direction of the currency movement. The importer wants a strong domestic currency to make the goods it imports less expensive. The exporter, on the other hand, wants exactly the opposite. It wants a weak domestic currency to make its goods more attractive to its foreign customers.

In the vast currency trading marketplace, these two types of businesses find each other, and join together in a way that is mutually beneficial. While one business may improve its competitiveness, it may lose money on the contract itself. The other loses business competitiveness but gains on the contract itself.

So, each is protected somewhat through this common ground. Of course, the same concept works among companies globally.

Forward currency contracts

One way in which firms can use foreign exchange markets to hedge risk is through the use of forward currency contracts, which are similar in many ways to futures contracts. This is best seen by an example. Suppose a U.S. electronics retailer knows that in 30 days it must pay yen to a Japanese TV manufacturer to ship the latest model of TVs to them, which they will sell at $1000 each. This price is printed in their latest catalog, so it is fixed ahead of time and cannot be changed. The U.S. firm agrees to pay ¥90,000 per TV to the Japanese firm, so the profit is going to depend on the dollar-yen exchange rate. If the exchange rate is ¥100 to $1 (which is $0.01 per yen), then each TV costs the U.S. firm $900, and they make $100 profit on each one they sell.

However, due to other deals and funds that the U.S. firm is waiting to complete and receive, it does not have the funds to buy the TVs right now. If over the next 30 days, the dollar suddenly depreciates to ¥85 per dollar (or $0.012 per yen), then each TV costs the U.S. retailer $1059 per TV, and it will actually lose $59 each time a U.S. customer buys one. To hedge against this exchange rate risk, the retailer can make a 30-day forward exchange deal with its bank, who agrees to sell yen to it in 30 days at a rate of $0.0105 per yen. This equates to $945 per TV, which would be a profit of $55 per TV. By making this forward deal, the U.S. firm has guaranteed making a profit, and has insured itself against the possibility of a sudden exchange rate change that will turn a profitable deal into a loss.

Exporting inflation

Think back to the earlier example of dollars being traded for euros in order for a U.S. citizen to purchase a German product. Does everybody win? The U.S. citizen gets a better bargain and the German seller gets a sale. But this is likely not the end of the story. Generally speaking, leaders of countries (politicians) are naturally always looking to improve their respective economies. If a country's domestic economy is performing satisfactorily but there is excess capacity available, whereby actual output is falling somewhere below potential, why not find a way to increase exports and expand the economy and GDP further? As long as it doesn't push too far and create an inflationary environment, it makes sense. All else being equal, here's how:

Suppose a country, we'll call it ABC, endeavors to expand its exports and chooses to use monetary policy as a stimulus. ABC's central bank feeds reserves into the banking system through open-market operations, essentially purchasing government bonds from commercial banks in exchange for new reserves which it creates out of nothing. The newly pumped-up reserve balance will sit in the bank's account at the central bank so those funds will not actually filter out into the economy. However, the inflated reserve pool will drive the central bank's target interest rate down, which will serve to increase lending activity and create new deposits which begin circulating in the private sector. And that new money creation will result in more money serving ABC's economy, decreasing the value of each unit of its currency (depreciation), as there are now more units out there chasing goods (see Figure 6.4).

Looking a bit deeper, the currencies decrease in value quickly as currency markets know that, over time, this rapid growth in money supply will outpace growth in actual output, causing inflation, as those with money will compete with each other for the available output that they want or need, driving up prices. At that point, their goods are too expensive in the global marketplace, and they now have purchasing power disparity. As demand for goods drops, demand for the currency also drops, as does its value. Thus, those in the currency trading business, primarily banks, in order to avoid loss in particular currencies, begin to reprice them downward by selling those currencies or entering into various derivative contracts for protection.

Over time, of course, GDP will grow as a result of new productive investment. But in the short term, the relatively sudden increase of money in

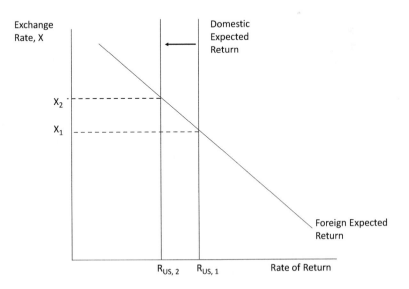

Figure 6.4 Decrease in Domestic Interest Rate Effect on Exchange Rate.

circulation will have a direct impact on the value of ABC's currency. And this impact will spread to other countries by way of the foreign exchange market. Now that other currencies are relatively more valuable, those countries' citizens will be more likely to purchase goods from ABC. That may go on for a short time, but as those countries eventually begin losing exports to ABC, their central banks may take similar action and attempt to influence currency values to their advantage.

It is common sense, really. As other countries' purchasing power of ABC's exports increases and they begin to realize a decrease in their exports, they have two choices. Either (1) they allow their local currency to continue to rise relative to ABC's and, thereby, continue to suffer losses of exports or (2) their central bank can take action to counter the currency's rise by stimulating an increase in their money supply. While initially addressing the exchange differential, the increase in the money supply will also create inflationary pressure. This is the meaning of the term *exporting inflation*. The actions taken by ABC's central bank resulted in a knock-on effect, whereby another country, through its own reactionary measures, ended up with inflation in its domestic economy. And the process will go back and forth as long as the countries are competing with each other, creating an overall tendency for worldwide inflation to creep up relative to worldwide GDP. Once the cycle begins, it is difficult to break.

So, now, looking back at the example of the dollar vs. euro valuation, let's suppose that the United States' Central Bank has executed stimulus measures intended to make the dollar more competitive. A German buyer would thus be encouraged to buy more U.S. goods, and thus, U.S. exports begin to rise, raising American GDP. But what about German producers of goods and services? They expect to now lose some of their business, because the U.S. goods are more competitively priced. In order to avoid a falling GDP, the German central bankers, as part of the Eurozone, will find a way to increase their own money supply, erasing this advantage.

While it is possible that this type of activity could take place between two countries, it is far more likely that many countries would be carrying out these money games against each other. As the money supply of these countries gradually increases relative to GDP, the inflationary pressure will be felt by the worldwide banking system. So, while exporting inflation might not seem significant on a global scale when it happens to one country, the fact that it is a phenomenon that can affect all of the largest economies in the world at the same time makes it an international concern.

The Eurozone and its problems

Having used the United States and Germany in the above examples, let's talk about the Eurozone, itself a trading bloc. Formed on January 1, 1999, the Eurozone is comprised of 19 European area member countries: Belgium, Germany, Ireland, Spain, France, Italy, Luxembourg, the Netherlands, Austria,

Portugal, Finland, Greece, Slovenia, Cyprus, Malta, Slovakia, Estonia, and Latvia. Note that the Eurozone is officially known as Europe's Economic and Monetary Union (EMU). This is a subset of countries that together form the European Union (EU)—in other words, there are members of the EU who are not yet in EMU, such as Denmark and Sweden. The purpose was to create a trading bloc of countries unified by a common new currency, the euro, to increase trade with each other and with the entire world.

In economics, it is widely known that the use of one currency can significantly increase trade. The widespread benefits are logical: avoiding the transaction costs of exchanging currencies in the market, through Forex, as well as the knowledge that one currency used within that trading bloc will not deviate in value from the time a transaction is contracted until it is completed. However, while originally conceived as a cure for fragmented Europe's economic ills, it has not been universally respected in idea or practice. Many economists believe there is a fundamental flaw. While monetary policy is coordinated through one central bank, the European Central Bank (ECB), based in Frankfurt, Germany, a unified fiscal policy (government spending, regulation, etc.) was never fully implemented.

Primarily controlled by the governing bodies of each of the 19 Eurozone members, there is no strong and unified agreement regarding governmental fiscal behavior among the Eurozone members. This problem becomes painfully apparent when some countries economically out-perform others and when some governments spend more, tax more, and borrow more than others. Think of Greece's 2009 debt crisis to be reminded of the economic chaos engulfing the Eurozone in this era.

If economists are beginning to understand the need for common fiscal governance, can we expect to see eventual economic success for the Eurozone nations? While anything is possible, it will take more than willing participants to solve the flaws in their union. In addition to the lack of fiscal unity, which is huge, the countries are faced with currency and budgetary constraints that stem from the fact that the individual members of the monetary union are not issuers of the currency that they use. In that way, they are much like states in the United States. Yet, we are different in that our states are all members of one monetary union with one national fiscal policy and a single Treasury that oversees monetary actions and is responsible for the production of the currency that we use.

As an issuer of its own currency, the United States has the ability to manage budgetary shortfalls through Treasury security issuances with the assurance that it will not default. While it may be inflationary, a currency issuer can always produce the money needed to settle its debts. Because the Eurozone member nations have no ability to issue currency, they are faced with the real possibility of defaulting on debt, forcing borrowing from other member nations, and others, and possibly straining relations.

A theory that economists often apply to cases such as the United States and the Eurozone is the theory of Optimum Currency Areas (OCAs). If two countries conduct a lot of trade—both in terms of volume and of scope—and the factors of production (labor and capital) are mobile across these countries, then it can make sense for them to share a common currency. An example of this is the states of the United States. On the other hand, if some, but not all, of these factors are in place, the OCA theory does not apply. For example, the United States and Japan conduct a lot of trade—in terms of the number of goods and the types of goods—but the geographic distance makes it very difficult for workers to move easily between the two economies. Thus, sharing a common currency would not be beneficial. Given the shared currency between countries that make up the Eurozone, we assume it is an Optimum Currency Area. However, there is evidence suggesting labor does not move as much as we may think across Europe, which thus casts doubt as to whether the Eurozone really constitutes an OCA.

Further limitations on Eurozone nations' monetary autonomy come into play, ironically, due to the same fixed rate exchange system that was designed to benefit trade. A floating exchange rate system allows a country to implement policies to increase or reduce its money supply and, thereby, affect economic conditions such as interest rates and inflation. On the other hand, a country that has a fixed exchange rate now can only use interest rate policy to maintain its fixed exchange rate and cannot independently seek to alter its exchange rate in order to alter imports or exports. The widely varying rates of productivity among the Eurozone members, even when disciplined by purchasing power parity in the marketplace, makes a unified currency a difficult objective to maintain. And, without unified fiscal policies or a common finance ministry, the Eurozone countries are prevented from working toward a common goal and, despite being part of the same union, in many ways they are as much competitors as they are teammates.

With that bit of background, it becomes easier to see why the use of a single currency for purposes of trade has not provided the benefit the Eurozone countries were seeking. Each country is implementing the fiscal measures that it deems prudent to attempt to regulate its own economy. And because it is tethered to the other countries in its monetary union, it is affected by the policies being carried out by its fellow trading partners. Alliances between countries inevitably form, sometimes for mutual benefit in dealing with certain matters and other times simply to survive, and the lack of a common goal with unified focus makes it difficult for the union to thrive.

Although the member nations are in some ways like the states of America, the shared history is very different, and the cultural differences between European countries are arguably greater than the variations between American states. Even if the Eurozone were to eventually implement fiscal unity in name, its member nations may still differ widely along many different dimensions. And that may be the biggest hurdle they must overcome if they are to achieve the economic success they desire. Indeed, the different political ideologies, histories, languages, and cultures of the countries in Europe make it hard to see whether further integration will be successful.

Global economy

Everyone is aware of the way our modern world is connected. The internet allows us to communicate globally in real time, making it possible to do business in ways previous generations would have never dreamed possible. This connectivity also presents us with challenges in terms of the way national economies are impacted by one another. The foreign exchange market is a prime example of the way technology has opened the doors for the development of a new business model. And the affect that the market has on world currency values is not to be underestimated. Even if we do not participate in the market, we should understand how it works in order to makes sense of our economic universe.

Just as we all play a part in our local economy, each country is a part of the global economy. And whether by governmental action or by business practices, the world's nations affect one another. When one country exports inflation, or when some governments over borrow, it tends to create worldwide tolerance for greater and greater government debt, leading to the likelihood of that debt becoming more burdensome on a less rapidly expanding world GDP.

As anyone who has gone through a recession can testify, if a country, or the whole world, becomes over leveraged, future problems loom. It is a question not only of debt but also of living standards. Can we grow GDP faster to rebalance the economy? Can we reduce government spending as the cure? Should we employ a combination of both? We must look at the big picture.

The world is changing faster that some can keep up with. Technology and innovation are the driving forces behind much economic advancement. And as the economies of emerging countries begin to grow faster, led by innovation, the global economy must adapt. Rapid changes in allocation and utilization of world resources can already be seen, affecting the supply and demand equilibrium. As economic standards rise for more people, the expectation of a higher standard of living will develop. Businesses will adapt quickly and address the demands that will stem from these expectations.

Governments must proceed cautiously, as global interconnectivity means that even seemingly tiny policy changes have greater capacity to impact not only a country's citizens but also the world. Currency values are at the heart of almost every economic issue, both domestic and foreign. Even the slightest shifts in value can have worldwide impact. And in this age of instant communication, the effects of news can translate into changes in currency markets almost immediately. And again, confidence is key: maybe even more so at the global level!

More than ever, we must be aware of how interconnected our world has become. If we are to be part of the global economy, we must think and act globally. We must consider the impact that our choices will have on not only ourselves but also on the world. And that begins with true economic understanding.

Key terms

- **Foreign Exchange**—the market where buyers and sellers trade currencies.
- **Exchange Rate**—the price of one currency in terms of another.
- **Interest Parity Condition**—the equation that solves for the market's equilibrium exchange rate.
- **Arbitrage**—when trading occurs between markets when a good or service is priced differently, where the trades then bring prices into parity.
- **Purchasing Power Parity**—the theory that tells us that the exchange rate is the ratio of prices in one country relative to another.
- **Forward Exchange Contracts**—an agreement to buy or sell currency at an agreed upon future date for a pre-determined exchange rate.
- **Optimum Currency Area**—a specific area, usually geographic, where a single currency would provide the greatest economic benefit to member nations.
- **Eurozone**—a subset of European Union countries that share the same currency, the euro, and have a shared monetary policy.

End-of-chapter problems

1. Consider the British pound-U.S. dollar exchange rate, where £1 currently trades for $1.3. There is a British citizen who wants to buy an American pair of jeans that retails for $50, while an American consumer wishes to purchase a British soccer jersey for £75.

   a. Calculate the price of jeans for the British consumer in pounds.
   b. Calculate the price of the soccer jersey for the American consumer in dollars.
   c. Re-do the calculations from (a) and (b), but where the pound depreciates to $1.2 per British pound.

2. The U.S. interest rate is 5%, the Japanese interest rate is 12%, the dollar-yen exchange rate is ¥100 per $1, and we expect it will be ¥110 per $1 in a year's time.

   a. Over the period of this year, do investors prefer U.S. bonds or Japanese bonds?
   b. What value of the exchange rate makes investors indifferent between both of these countries' bonds?

3. Using the foreign exchange rate diagram:

   a. Show what happens to the equilibrium exchange rate if the domestic country lowers their interest rate.
   b. What if there is expected depreciation at the same time that the interest rate was lowered?

4. What might happen to the exchange rate if both the home and foreign countries simultaneously raised their interest rates at the same time? Does the magnitude of the interest rate change matter?

5. A pair of sneakers sells for $80 in the United States and €60 in Europe:

   a. What should the exchange rate be according to PPP?
   b. Suppose the dollar-euro exchange rate is actually €1 to $1.2. Based on this market exchange rate, is the dollar over- or under-valued according to PPP?

6. Describe the practical reasons why arbitrage cannot always be exploited when there is a price difference in different markets for the same identical product.

7. An individual exchanges $1000 for £760 in the morning, and then exchanges their pounds back into dollars at the end of the day where the exchange rate is £1 to $1.4. Calculate how many dollars this individual is left with at the end of the day.

8. Go back to the numerical example of the foreign currency contract in this question.

   a. If the exchange rate changed to ¥120 per $1, what is the amount of profit that the U.S. electronics retailer can make on each item sold?
   b. What type of financial instrument can they target in order to preserve potential gains in the movement of the exchange rate?

9. A large country decides to cut money supply and reduce inflation. Using the theory developed in this chapter, explain whether this could cause a reduction in inflation in other countries in the world as well.

10. Two countries neighbor each other and have different currencies.

   a. If both countries trade only one product with each other, albeit in vast quantities, do they constitute an optimum currency area?
   b. What if they trade a vast amount of product and in large volumes too, although workers in these countries do not ever wish to move. Are they an optimum currency area?

7 Monetary sterilization in China

Objectives

1. To learn what monetary sterilization is, how it operates, and why it is sometimes used.
2. The unique operation of monetary sterilization in China is studied.
3. The accounting entries to a central bank's balance sheet that sterilizes is presented.

The topic of currency manipulation is one that has come up repeatedly over the past many years, particularly among discussions and commentaries about the relationship between China and the United States. As we can see in the following chart (Figure 7.1), China has often sought to fix their exchange rate. We see this strongly in the period of 1994–2005, where the China-United States exchange rate does not move at all. China then relaxed their hold on the exchange rate until 2014, and since then have since loosely kept their exchange rate within a certain range.

This chapter is about *monetary sterilization*, a practice that is largely unknown to most people, yet has been actively implemented in China in recent decades. This probably hurts the rest of the developed world and could eventually damage China itself.

There is disagreement as to the real impact of monetary intervention, largely due to a lack of fundamental understanding, and it should be pointed out that China is not alone in carrying on forms of this practice. Currency intervention has been used by many countries, including the United States, Korea, Japan, Switzerland, and others who reportedly use forms of it today in an attempt to manage the value of their currency in the foreign exchange markets. So, why do we care so much about China's practice and its impact on the world? Well, partly due to the size of China's economy. But primarily because it appears to give them an undue advantage with regard to trade. And when one of the largest economies in the world operates this way, the impact is far reaching. Given the ever-growing amounts of Chinese exports that countries seek, the practice could be particularly punitive to exporters in the rest of the world.

Before we dig into the practice of monetary sterilization, first consider a real-world example. Both of the authors have worked and lived in North

DOI: 10.4324/9781003251453-9

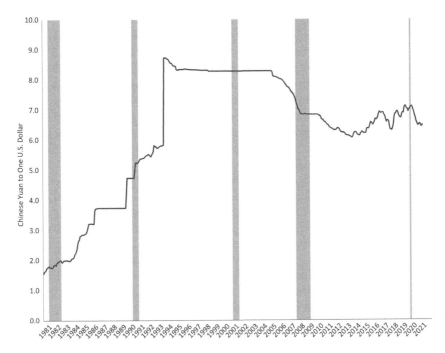

Figure 7.1 China/United States Exchange Rate.
Source: Board of Governors of the Federal Reserve

Carolina, at least for some portion of their lives, which has traditionally had a strong furniture manufacturing industry. Some years ago, the majority of the state's furniture manufacturing firms began to seriously contract. Their sales began to fall, and profits followed in a downward spiral—more quickly than one could have ever imagined. One after another, furniture manufacturing plants soon began going out of business. These companies had prospered for years, some for generations, and within less than two decades, they were shutting their doors, leaving behind a multitude of empty factory buildings.

Comparative advantage and foreign competition

The economic law of *comparative advantage* helps explain what happened. In a nutshell, it is very simply this: there are two countries, and each produces two goods. Relatively speaking, country 1 is more efficient at making good A than good B, and country 2 is more efficient at making good B than good A. The theory of comparative advantage shows that both countries are better off if country 1 produces good A and country 2 produces good B, and then they trade, with each country benefitting from the other's specialization. It is important to note that this theory holds true even if one of the countries can produce <u>both</u> goods at less cost than the other country in absolute terms (known as *absolute* advantage).

To see the difference between comparative and absolute advantage in a simpler and more microeconomic way, consider this example. There are two neighbors who live next door to each other: one house has a family that includes a 15-year-old boy, and the other house is lived in and owned by Serena Williams. Serena Williams is a physically gifted individual and is arguably one of the greatest athletes of all time across any sport. Next, consider the time it takes them to cut the grass: Serena Williams could mow her lawn much faster and easier than the teenage boy could. Therefore, she has the absolute advantage when it comes to yard work.

Yet, she would be better off using her time to instead play in a tennis tournament or to film a sneaker commercial for Nike. In other words, even though she has the absolute advantage when it comes to cutting the grass, she is still better off hiring the teenage boy to cut the grass instead. Comparatively—with regard to the relative cost of his time—it is less costly for him to do the job. So, the teenage boy actually has the comparative advantage when it comes to doing the yard work. This is also how it operates internationally when considering trade between nations: it is not about who has the lowest *absolute* costs, but about who has the lowest *comparative* costs.

China's comparative advantage has been the relatively low wages of its workers as compared with workers from the rest of the world. As China industrialized and brought in very low paid workers from their farms and trained them for factory work, the nation quickly became an industrial giant. But the magnitude of its comparative advantage was simply breath-taking.

Currency sterilization

The term 'currency sterilization' refers to the practice of intervening in the foreign exchange markets with the intention of maintaining the value of one currency relative to another, while also attempting to curb growth in the monetary base. Remember from the foreign exchange market diagram developed in the previous chapter that a country cannot change its interest rate without expecting a resulting exchange rate change. Yet, a country that is fixing their exchange rate would like to get hold of as many foreign assets as possible in order to maintain their fixed exchange rate. Sterilization allows them to do this.

Typically, intervention takes place when a central bank purchases foreign currency from its commercial bank system, paying for it by issuing new reserves, resulting in an increase in the domestic monetary base. If that central bank wishes to reverse that injection of new base money (i.e. addition to reserves), it must then employ tactics to adjust out the newly issued reserves, thereby *sterilizing* the change created by the intervention. Let us now see this process a little more precisely by means of an example.

Suppose the Chinese central bank has the following simple balance sheet:

Assets	Liabilities
Domestic Assets 4 trillion	Currency 2 trillion Reserves 2 trillion

where the vast majority of domestic assets held by the central bank are domestic bonds. Notice that the liabilities side—currency plus reserves—is equivalent to the monetary base. Next, suppose there is increasing pressure on China's currency, such that it would appreciate if the central bank did not intervene. For example, this could be caused by a greater supply of foreign currencies—such as the U.S. dollar—on the market. The issue for China—the country trying to maintain its exchange rate—is that if these foreign currencies are not removed through intervention, they are available for trade on the foreign exchange market. This enlarged pool of foreign currencies makes the yuan more valuable relative to them, which is not what China desires since it raises the prices of their goods that are exported overseas. This thereby makes Chinese goods less competitive, which is the very thing they wish to avoid.

To counteract the influx of foreign currency to the foreign exchange market—and to maintain the current value of their currency—the Chinese central bank purchases foreign currency:

Assets	Liabilities
Domestic Assets 4 trillion Foreign Currency (U.S.D) 200 billion	Currency 2 trillion Reserves 2 trillion New Reserves 200 billion

where the foreign currency is paid for by adding to the reserve accounts of commercial banks in China. Notice that if we stop there, the monetary base will have risen. However, the central bank counteracts this by swapping the new reserves for newly issued domestic sterilization bonds, which serves to nullify the previous increase in reserves.

Assets	Liabilities
Domestic Assets 4 trillion Foreign Currency (U.S.D) 200 billion	Currency 2 trillion Reserves 2 trillion Domestic Sterilization Bonds 200 billion

This last act is the essence of sterilization, where the central bank has acted to prevent a change in the monetary base, all the while maintaining its desired level for the exchange rate.

So, sterilization is the second part of a two-step process. In China's case, it essentially involves efforts to control the exchange rate between the yuan and the U.S. dollar in order to maintain the competitive advantage that the country currently enjoys, combined with the efforts by the Chinese central bank to control the supply of base money. It is a complex process that is hindered by the fact that China's release of data to the rest of the world is not done freely. This lack of transparency leads to speculation based on 'circumstantial evidence,' as is apparent in the widely divergent information that can be gleaned from reputable publications. Combined with the misunderstandings of the way the modern banking system operates, the lack of reliable information serves to produce reports which leave us with more questions than answers. So, while we do not clearly understand all of the finer nuances of the practices carried out by the Chinese central bank, we have enough information, supported by corroborating evidence, to develop an idea of how China sterilizes its currency.

Most politicians and journalists, and unfortunately many economists, miss the distinction between intervention and sterilization, therefore they do not understand that the second step is the problem. It is a technical process that, quite frankly, can only be made clear with a working knowledge of modern banking and the fundamentals of a double-entry system of accounting. And while we can examine the technical aspects of the way currency sterilization is carried out, we should attempt to understand the motives behind the actions, as that is the real concern.

Sterilization policy emanates from the monetarist theory that expansion in the money supply creates inflation. And when a country is experiencing large inflows of foreign capital into its domestic economy from export sales, excessive inflation is a valid concern. By controlling domestic inflation, China is able to suppress the natural rise in price levels that would result from its long-running trade surplus. But it comes at a price. The exploding growth in its exports, combined with its intervention in the foreign exchange markets, has resulted in quite a conundrum for China.

To illustrate how it appears that China is manipulating its currency and to distinguish between intervention and sterilization, we can look at an example:

> Suppose a Chinese manufacturer sells 1 million U.S. dollars' worth of goods to an American company. The Chinese economy is closed in terms of currency acceptance (called *capital controls*), requiring anyone doing business with Chinese companies to exchange their native currency for yuan. So, the American company will go to the foreign exchange market, typically by way of a Chinese commercial bank, and exchange its 1 million U.S. dollars for an equivalent amount of yuan. Two things have happened. One, money was transferred from the U.S. to China in exchange for goods. Since the dollars were exchanged for yuan, which was already outstanding in the Chinese economy, the net

increase in wealth is held in the form of U.S. dollars which are sitting on the Chinese commercial bank's balance sheet as reserves from foreign exchange. And, two, the supply (think of it as inventory) of dollars vs. yuan in the foreign exchange market has now shifted, resulting in a natural change in the relative value of the two currencies.

The introduction of more dollars into the foreign exchange market decreases the value of the dollar, thereby making the yuan relatively more valuable than before. A weaker dollar would alter American demand for Chinese goods as well as making American goods more affordable for foreign purchasers. The reduction in demand for Chinese exports is made more severe by the boost to American manufacturers, a double impact that China doesn't desire, which is why they pursue currency *intervention*. In order to maintain the targeted exchange rate, and secure the Chinese balance of trade relative to U.S. manufacturers, the People's Bank of China (PBOC), which is the central bank of China, will purchase the $1 million dollars that went into the foreign exchange market and it will do so with newly issued yuan. The PBOC is essentially executing a swap with the commercial bank by taking the $1 million dollars held in foreign reserves and giving the bank new yuan reserves in exchange. This surge in foreign reserves can be good for the PBOC in the sense that it needs dollars to maintain the chosen pegged exchange rate, and it can meet foreign debt obligations too. Yet, the problem is that without acting further, money supply will rise, which could be inflationary, and actually could alter the very exchange rate the country is trying to maintain, so the central bank intervenes.

The commercial bank's balance sheet position is restored, with no change in net worth, and the PBOC's balance sheet has now expanded. In doing this, the PBOC is essentially keeping the value of the yuan *pegged* or fixed against the value of the U.S. dollar. With that accomplished, the PBOC could effectively leave the intervention there and know that it preserved the exchange rate at its desired target. However, Chinese officials fear that prices would rise in the domestic economy as a result of the newly issued base money, believing that it would spur new lending. (Actually, the increase in deposits is really just a response to the new wealth that came into the country by way of the export sale.) *Sterilization* is the prescribed course of action to remove the newly issued liquidity (base money) and the PBOC executes this step typically with a form of open market operations, whereby it swaps domestic bonds, often referred to as sterilization bonds, for the newly issued yuan reserves.

Let's review those steps in the context of sterilization. The classic definition of monetary sterilization is currency intervention that attempts to prevent the actions of a central bank from resulting in an increase in the monetary base. And when the PBOC purchased the dollars by issuing new yuan reserves, the monetary base was increased by that amount. So, to counter, or sterilize, the increase in base money, the PBOC must somehow remove the extra yuan that it created. This is most often done either through open market operations, similar to the way the Fed alters the reserve pool, or by raising the reserve requirements placed on commercial banks. With open market operations, the central bank sells domestic bonds to the commercial banks, thereby removing the base money from the pool. If reserve requirements are raised, it would theoretically increase the amounts, calculated as a percentage of their deposits, that the commercial banks are required to hold at the central bank, essentially suppressing the circulation of the reserves between banks.

Both of these methods are attempts at removing base money from the reserve pool, in an effort to negate the effects of foreign exchange intervention, with an added intention of limiting the amount of reserves circulating in the banking system to support lending activities. And if you are attempting to curb price inflation, as triggered by growth in your broad money supply, you would first look to reduce the rate at which banks are making new loans.

If you recall the discussion from our chapter on money creation earlier in the book, much of the previous illustration probably sounds contradictory to the notion that lending is not constrained by reserves. It is contradictory because, quite simply, it appears that the Chinese, like many classically educated economists in the United States and around the world, do not understand the actual mechanics of the modern banking system. Although we do not have particular statements to this effect, it seems clear in the obvious adherence to the idea that the money supply expands when banks lend based on a money multiplier. While PBOC officials do not explicitly state that they are attempting to stem lending *of* reserves, their actions do imply that they believe that lending is reserve constrained. So, while we cannot discuss the methods that the PBOC uses in its sterilization practices without implying this theory, one should keep in mind the differences between its approach and what we know to be true in the U.S. banking system.

While classical economic teachings promote ideas such as the money multiplier or the loanable funds model, both of which we know to be based on the premise that lending is dependent on existing deposits, not all of such theories are entirely erroneous. Some just do not apply to way the modern banking system actually works. For example, increases in the money supply can be inflationary but the root of those increases does not lie in a money multiplier because banks do not lend deposits and lending is not reserve constrained. But that does not diminish the concern for inflation. Rather than discard the entire idea, those who truly understand the modern monetary system suggest modification in approach, making the macroeconomic theories more relevant by boiling them down to mechanics in order to effectively apply them to the system within which we currently operate.

With that said, we can return to our illustration. Regardless of method, we know that China's primary goal is to maintain its competitive manufacturing advantage by artificially fixing the relative exchange rate of the yuan to the dollar and preventing inflation in its domestic economy. It is clear that, whether by open market operations or raising reserve requirements, the PBOC is attempting to sterilize the increases in its monetary base that occur as it issues new yuan reserves to buy the U.S. dollars that enter into the foreign exchange market. Essentially, the foreign exchange balance is constantly upset, as China continues its pattern of net exports, requiring the PBOC to undertake intervention actions to restore the balance.

These transactions appear to take place, literally, on a daily basis, as the PBOC aims to maintain its control of the relative exchange value of the yuan to the dollar. It doesn't take a big imagination to entertain the volume of sterilizing actions required to counter these continued injections of yuan. In fact, we know that the PBOC has routinely carried out open market operations at a minimum of twice each week, often to the tune of hundreds of billions of yuan, to adjust the liquidity in the banking system's reserves.

While the recent recessionary times have led the PBOC to inject reserves *into* the banking system, open market operations have typically been used to drain the liquid foreign exchange reserves which result from intervention. The resulting build-up in domestic bonds on Chinese commercial bank balance sheets translates into mounting interest costs that the PBOC must find a way to pay. Now, the PBOC is certainly not without resources. But what about all the U.S. dollars purchased by the PBOC through its intervention practices? Resting in the PBOC's foreign exchange reserve coffers, the dollars are a non-income producing asset.

In an attempt to offset the interest cost of the ever-increasing volume of outstanding domestic *sterilization* bonds, the PBOC often converts the foreign reserve dollars into income producing assets by using them to purchase U.S. Treasury securities, a relatively safe asset backed by the U.S. government and one that is denominated in dollars, so the purchases do not affect the balance of foreign exchange. When you hear or read that the United States is in debt to China, this is what the journalists are referring to. And while there are theories of sinister motives or underlying plans to control the U.S. economy, the build-up of Treasury holdings by the Chinese can be directly tied to the PBOC's currency intervention and sterilization operations.

What about the money supply?

With all of this focus on reserves, it may seem that the PBOC has lost sight of the overall money supply. After all, the monetary base, as we know, simply circulates within the banking system as reserves. Money creation happens when banks expand their balance sheets with newly created deposits resulting from new lending. But, what about the new deposits that are likely occurring as a result of the sales being made by Chinese exporters? Aren't those deposits creating money?

They do increase China's M2, which we know is defined as the total of bank deposits, short-term savings accounts, time deposits, and the like. But, M2 changes constantly as deposits move in and out of banks as part of normal business operations. So, while each deposit into a bank increases M2 at that point, the money being deposited was already in existence and was withdrawn from some bank at some other point in time, whereby it decreased M2. If the deposit moved from a foreign bank into a Chinese bank, it is just shifting from one place to another. Since there is no new extension of credit associated with the deposit, the overall global money supply does not increase.

However, since this does increase money in circulation in China, it can be inflationary in the Chinese economy. And it should, theoretically, be inflationary if it is in response to increases in productivity and GDP. As money moves into the country when it sells its exports abroad, productivity and GDP rise. As long as this rise is a natural evolution of healthy, moderate growth, it should be a seen as a positive occurrence. In fact, the healthy growth that results from productivity is what keeps an economy moving forward.

Regardless of perception toward inflation and growth, the basic truth is that in order for an economy to expand, the money supply must grow through the banking system by extensions of new credit. So, while the PBOC might be undertaking the classic approaches to controlling growth in the money supply, it is accurate in its apparent focus on slowing the rate of lending by commercial banks.

If you understand the fundamentals of the modern banking system, you must be wondering why the PBOC seems to concentrate on using open market operations and high reserve requirements as its primary tools to manage the monetary base in an effort to control lending. This seems to imply, again, that the PBOC's approach is based on a belief in the money multiplier. In the modern banking system, lending is not reserve constrained. Capital requirements are the limiting factor for banks making new loans. If the banking system wished to slow lending, an increase in capital requirements would be almost instantly effective.

Another logical step would be to address credit qualification standards. And, in fact, the PBOC has at times implemented more stringent loan qualification policies, sometimes requiring as much as 40%–50% in down payments for new borrowing (this is particularly effective in stemming new housing loans) and enforcing credit quotas that result in rationing the extension of new lending. So, while we know that addressing reserve requirements and monetary base changes in the United States would not have much effect on lending beyond an impact on the Fed Funds rate, we can really only make assumptions about the Chinese banking environment. Maybe the PBOC is using many tools and these are simply the most apparent. Perhaps the PBOC is simply attempting to control the interbank lending rate (their version of a Fed Funds rate) to suppress lending activities and using any means available to do so, although the required reserve ratio would have little to no impact in a system that has abundant reserves.

Perhaps banking regulations there cause the overall approach to reserve management to be different. For example, while we have no indication that this is the case, if the PBOC did not supply reserves as needed, banks would have difficulty in meeting stated requirements as they expanded their loan portfolios. And increases in the reserve requirements would accelerate the severity of that impact. Initially, the interbank lending rate would skyrocket and ultimately a credit crisis could ensue. Of course, there would be other fallout and the entire system would be in turmoil, giving us reason to assume that the PBOC has not enacted such a policy.

The fact remains that reports are often conflicting and underlying motivations are not apparent. Therefore, absent solid data, we must make assumptions about the restrictions and policies that the PBOC has implemented in order to makes sense of the motives behind its selection of monetary tools in a banking system that is far from transparent.

It should be noted that, under increasing pressure from world economic forces, China has eased reserve requirements placed on some smaller banks. Of course, it is stated that the motivation is to generate new lending activities. While we know that to be a misunderstood relationship, it likely would have little impact even if it was relevant, as the changes in requirements have been very small and only apply to a fraction of the country's banks.

The impossible trinity

So, countries such as China who wish to manipulate their exchange rate for trade or other reasons must make a choice: do they allow capital to flow freely into their banking system, thereby losing autonomous control of monetary policy, or do they pursue independent monetary policy while limiting the flows of capital? History shows us that it is impossible to do both things while pegging the currency, which is a relationship that is known by economists as *the impossible trinity* (also known as the *Trilemma*). This states that it is impossible for a country to have monetary policy autonomy, a fixed exchange rate, and free capital flows all at the same time (see Figure 7.2):

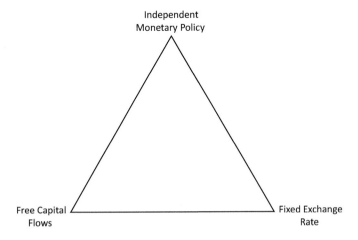

Figure 7.2 The Impossible Trinity.

For example, if a country allows market participants to freely buy or sell currency, while they simultaneously use interest rate policy for things like fighting inflation or stimulating the economy in a recession, then it will be impossible to fix the exchange rate. Likewise, if a country wants to maintain a fixed exchange rate and allow the free flow of capital, they will only be able to use monetary policy to offset changes in the supply and demand for currency in the foreign exchange market, and cannot change their interest rate to react to other macroeconomic shocks such as a fall in spending. In China's case, the main restraint they have elected to impose are capital controls. Their officials do not, therefore, allow financial flows to move freely into and out of the economy.

If moderate, sound growth is a sign of a healthy economy, why would Chinese officials be motivated to restrict growth by curbing lending? Wouldn't the government want to see its citizens' standard of living improve? Clearly, the country has enjoyed the competitive advantage achieved through keeping the value of the yuan artificially low. This advantage has resulted in dramatic growth in China's exports since the 1980s. It follows that the domestic economy would experience an increase in the money supply along with an expansion of such magnitude. Growth in the money supply, after all, is a natural result of an expanding GDP and a net exporter will experience growth as foreign currency comes into the economy in exchange for goods. But, as we know, if the money supply grows faster than GDP, which could happen if central bank actions were combined with economic expansion, excessive inflation can quickly follow, resulting in pressure on the yuan's value which could threaten the competitive advantage that the country desperately wants to continue to enjoy. Citing a fear of high inflation, the PBOC has placed its focus on keeping the value of the yuan artificially low while simultaneously fighting the battle of the increasing money supply.

Recession

While much of the PBOC's monetary policy activity remains shrouded in secrecy, more is being shared with the world and there are some things that we do understand to be true. As we have already covered, the PBOC seems to focus on credit creation in an attempt to control growth and it employs monetary policy to restrain inflation. We know that the PBOC has some of the same monetary tools at its disposal that the other central banks do, such as open market operations and making adjustments to the reserve requirement ratio, although the latter is not commonly used by many countries. And while the system is complicated by foreign exchange intervention and sterilization activities, we know that the PBOC targets interest rates in a similar way to that of many other central banks.

Though much of our discussion has focused on efforts to limit growth, it should be noted that China has not necessarily consistently restricted credit creation. In fact, China's 2008–2009 stimulus package, which was rolled out primarily in response to the global financial crisis, brought about a strong push toward rapid credit creation. The years between 2009 and 2011 saw increased pressures on Chinese officials to stabilize the economy. The reaction was to ramp up infrastructure and technological development projects in an effort to keep the economic engine churning ahead while at the same time tightening credit standards to curb lending in an attempt to prevent development of asset bubbles.

The years 2012 and 2013 were wrought with continued economic stress for China and the open market operations that continued twice per week often saw injections of liquidity into the banking system instead of draining reserves by swapping bonds. This pushed lending rates down as reserve requirement ratios were reduced and credit standards were loosened, all in an effort to stimulate loan activity. Most of the new lending was directed toward the real estate sector in order to bolster prices and prevent deflation in the market, which many believed to be overbuilt.

Now, as we know, a reduction in interest rates and a desire by banks to lend does not automatically create demand. Without confidence, borrowers will not take on new debt. Hence, the reason the Fed's quantitative easing did little to spur new lending in the United States. With similar conditions in the Chinese banking system, especially after a long period of restricted credit, it would seem that easing policies during the stimulus would have brought borrowers in droves. When that didn't happen, the PBOC reportedly issued directives to the banks to lend, basically forcing them find ways to make new loans. As a result, credit was extended to local governments and government-owned entities to fund more new projects. And while financing new public projects may be beneficial and perfectly well justified, we should consider that data indicating increased lending activities—implying a healthy economy—would include loans that were not necessarily issued in the ordinary course of business. Further, the Chinese banking system reportedly became faced with defaults and write-offs of a significant chunk of the newly extended loans, placing more pressure on the PBOC to deal with economic fallout. This inefficient lending caused by PBOC directives could eventually cause severe asset bubbles, damaging the entire economy and fueling unrest.

That brings us to where we are today. The Western world, usually deemed to include North America, Europe, Australia, and other developed countries, has been forced to deal with the export juggernaut that China has become. Comparative advantage, the theory developed by economist David Ricardo, which we discussed in relation to the furniture industry, is imminently fair and good for the citizens of the world. It brings about Adam Smith's notion of the *division of labor*, and over time accelerates and expands global trade, lifting living standards everywhere.

Sterilization is a different theme altogether. In fairness to China, it has been practiced by others in the course of history, including the United States, which sterilized in the 1920s. At the time, Great Britain, like most countries, was on the gold standard. Cheaper American goods, made so partially by sterilization, brought many British pounds into U.S. banks. The United States promptly swapped them for British gold, leaving them no choice but to abandon the gold standard. This illustrates that Britain also had the problem of a fixed gold price that was inconsistent with its stock of gold reserves: it was too low. With better forethought, they should have chosen to devalue their gold price.

Although China is not the first to employ sterilization tactics, it likely has been harmful to its international trading partners because of the size and importance of the Chinese economy as well as the duration of its sterilization program. The build-up in foreign reserves, held in U.S. currency as well as U.S. Treasury securities, on the PBOC balance sheet is evidence of its prolific sterilization actions. But the explosive rate of accumulation of foreign reserves cannot be maintained indefinitely, as there are extrinsic costs to the country.

Corollary effects

China's sterilization practices result in the build-up of dollars in the PBOC's foreign exchange reserve coffers. Because those dollars would otherwise just sit there, out of circulation, the PBOC deploys them into income producing assets, namely U.S. Treasury securities. By purchasing Treasury bonds, the Chinese government is deploying otherwise stagnant reserves into income producing securities which are backed by the American government. While the interest earned on the bonds serves to offset some of the cost of domestic sterilization bonds, purchasing the U.S. Treasury securities provides the PBOC with an additional means of control over the value of the dollar (strong demand for U.S. Treasuries maintains their value and, thus, the value of the dollar itself). This helps to manage the yuan to dollar exchange rate.

The build-up in China's portfolio of U.S. Treasury Bonds can be clearly seen in data published by the United States Department of the Treasury. While previously a significant player, China moved into the position of the largest foreign holder of U.S. national debt in 2008. It likely was a measure by Chinese officials to help stabilize the dollar-yuan exchange rate in order to boost exports.

As the largest holder of U.S. Treasury securities, China is in a particularly powerful position with respect to the U.S. economy. The Chinese government has accumulated a tremendous store of U.S. dollar-denominated assets and more are still being purchased. The longstanding trade imbalance has flooded the Chinese economy with U.S. dollars which, through sterilization, make their way to the PBOC. And, since we know that these dollars are used to purchase Treasury bonds, we understand that they find their way back into circulation in the U.S.

They are being used to purchase bonds, which is just an asset swap. But the dollars represent current spending power that is being exchanged for future spending power. And those dollars do find their way into the U.S. economy, returning that current spending power, which could be inflationary. Further, some assert that the large level of national debt in the United States is evidence of reckless spending practices. Thus, the PBOC's hungry appetite for Treasury bonds encourages deficit spending, adding to the ire that many U.S. politicians have sometimes harbored toward China.

However, we must add that although China holds a vast sum of U.S. Treasury bonds, they are unlikely to try to sell them all at once. Doing so would flood the market with these bonds, lowering their price, and thus lowering the value of China's holding of these Treasury bonds. In other words, trying to sell these bonds all at once would actually hurt, rather than help, China.

Shadow banks

While the portrayal of shadow banks as a sort of black market of the banking world is not altogether inaccurate, this secondary banking system need not be an enigma. Called shadow banks because they operate 'in the shadow' of the commercial banking system, these lending houses emerged in response to the growing demand of Chinese citizens who were unable to borrow from traditional lenders. Basically, operating without any sort of regulatory oversight, they often impose high interest rates and severe punishment for default.

Faced with onerous loan requirements and credit standards that prevent even the most credit worthy borrowers from obtaining loans, Chinese citizens are often unable to borrow from commercial banks. Historically, it was common in Chinese society to borrow from family members or close acquaintances in order to buy a home or expand a business. As the Chinese economy began its rise, human nature simply manifested itself in the desires of average citizens to improve their lives. The resulting need for credit became the driving force behind the emergence of the shadow banking world that we read about.

Nothing more than financial intermediaries, shadow banks work to bring those who have money to lend together with those who wish to borrow. The ability to create money 'out of thin air' by the extension of new credit is a power that is unique to the commercial banking system. Since shadow banks are just facilitating the lending of funds from one party to another, they do not create new money by virtue of an accounting entry. They actually do lend deposits. So, while new loans are made, there is no increase in the money supply.

While there is justified concern for the potential of fueling asset bubbles, the only real economic effect of the shadow banks is an increase in the velocity of the money already in circulation. Suppose someone had money and they lent it to another who is using it to buy a home or build a business: rather than sit idle in an account or under a mattress, that money has changed hands and is circulating in the economy. This can drive productivity, but it does not increase the money supply, therefore it should not really impact the PBOC's efforts at currency sterilization.

Inflation or appreciation?

Although the foregoing discussion mentions that the PBOC pegs the yuan to the value of the dollar, that is no longer fully true. For some time, through its intervention operations, China kept its yuan pegged tightly to the U.S. dollar. Under intense pressure from the West to let the yuan *float* (letting international markets through Forex determine its value), in June of 2010, it began compromising somewhat by allowing the yuan to float upward in small increments within a range, over time. As an example, suppose a foreign country, say the United States, lowered its interest rate. This would shift the foreign expected return curve (from the Chinese perspective) downward, as seen in Figure 7.3.

In the past, China may have responded by also cutting their interest rate to $R_{C,2}$, which would maintain the exchange rate at their desired level X_1, fixed at its original rate. But under a floating regime, they simply allow the exchange rate to appreciate to X_2.

China has maintained that its goal is to manage inflation, which officials argue justifies past efforts at sterilization. But moderate inflation would be a natural occurrence in an economy growing at the rate China has over the past few decades. So, is their fear really too much inflation? Actually, prosperity drives up asset prices. Higher GDP pushes up the standard of living. Higher income creates higher values, but that is appreciation, not inflation. And it is not only normal but essential to sustain a healthy private sector in a growing economy. By preventing a natural rate of appreciation, China's efforts have led to a large trade imbalance, resulting in predictions of banking crises and market bubbles.

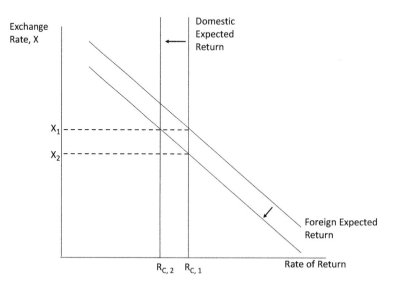

Figure 7.3 Maintaining a Fixed Exchange Rate.

Rapid, and arguably excessive, expansion in the export-driven economy has poured labor and other resources into that sector and prevented development of other areas of the domestic economy. Such is the cost of maintaining a super-competitive edge in manufacturing relative to its trading partners. China's officials have pursued their overall goal of keeping the value of the yuan artificially low against the dollar in order to perpetuate the advantage of lower labor and manufacturing costs, keeping the cost of Chinese products cheaper and, therefore, more attractive. They have successfully capitalized on this advantage for decades, but the inherent costs make their rate of sterilization unsustainable.

Perhaps, we are already seeing signs of tapering in some of the shifts in monetary tactics and slowdowns in economic output. Although there have been pressures from countries in the west and recessionary factors to deal with, the moves by the PBOC do seem to indicate that changes may be occurring. And, while China was not unique in dealing with economic recession in recent years, undoubtedly, the environment in which the PBOC found itself was developed over years of currency manipulation and restricted growth, adding complication to the efforts to find resolution.

Key terms

- **Currency Sterilization**—the practice of intervening in foreign exchange markets to fix the exchange rate and prevent growth in the supply of money.
- **Comparative Advantage**—a country's ability to produce a good or service at a lower opportunity cost than the countries it trades with.
- **Capital Controls**—measures taken by a government, central bank, or other regulatory institution to limit the flow of foreign capital into and out of the domestic economy.
- **Shadow Banking**—lending and other financial services conducted by institutions that are not regulated or under conditions that are unregulated.

End-of-chapter problems

1. Based on Figure 7.1, when did China make the biggest step to deliberately weaken the value of their currency?
2. Two people live in the same neighborhood, where one is an Olympic sprinter and the other is a teenager. The sprinter is faster at taking their dog for a walk than the teenager is. According to the theory of comparative advantage, should the sprinter take their dog for a walk or hire the teenager to do it in their place? Explain your answer.
3. A country chooses to cause depreciation of their currency.

   a. If the demand for their goods is very elastic, do exports sales go up or down?

    b.   What if the demand for their goods is very inelastic, do exports sales go up or down? Is there any other information we need to answer this question?

4. A central bank has 2,000 in domestic assets and 3,000 in foreign assets, with 1,500 currency in circulation and 3,500 in reserves.

    a.   Show what the central bank's balance sheet looks like.

    b.   Suppose the central bank sells 1,000 in domestic assets. Does money supply rise or fall?

    c.   What should the central bank do with foreign assets if it did not want money supply to change in (b)?

5. Draw the foreign exchange market diagram from 4(b) and 4(c) so to show how the interest rate and exchange rate move in this scenario.

6. Consider the Impossible Trinity:

    a.   Which two options has the United States selected?

    b.   Which two options were selected by countries (not the United States) under the Bretton-Woods agreement?

7. Suppose China owns billions of dollars' worth of U.S. Treasuries.

    a.   In a staggering move, they decide to buy just as many Treasuries today on the market. Drawing a supply and demand diagram, show what happens to the price of these bonds.

    b.   What has happened to the value of China's U.S. Treasury holdings following (a)?

8. Based on the discussion in this chapter, describe three economic policies you would like China to implement for the welfare of their citizens, assuming you were the chief economic advisor to the Chinese government?

8 World reserve currency

Objectives

1. To learn what a world reserve currency is and how and why the U.S. dollar has served in that role.
2. We examine the costs and benefits of a global reserve currency, from the perspective of the reserve country and from the perspective of other countries.
3. We will learn what the gold standard and reserve currency systems are.

A discussion of how the money supply works both within the United States and around the globe should include an understanding of the status of the U.S. dollar as the world's primary reserve currency. What does the term reserve currency mean? Why is it important? And how did the U.S. dollar become the world's reserve currency?

What does world reserve currency mean?

If you could travel back through history, you would see dominant currencies come and go in conjunction with the emergence and decline of world financial superpowers. Strictly speaking, a reserve currency is defined as one that is acceptable as a medium for settlement of international debts and therefore is held in reserve in large quantities by many countries. To attain reserve status, a currency must be viewed as having a stable long-term value and there must be a readily available supply of money and securities denominated in that currency. The U.S. dollar satisfies both of these requirements. In addition, many international contracts around the world are denominated in U.S. dollars, even when America is not involved. For example, Canada might buy $100 billion worth of oil from Saudi Arabia and pay in U.S. dollars, where both Canada and Saudi Arabia consider the dollar as a worthy means of payment. This feature makes the U.S. dollar attractive as world reserve currency.

The hallmarks of the dollar that make it especially suitable for the role are the strength of the U.S. economy and the depth and liquidity of the U.S.

DOI: 10.4324/9781003251453-10

financial market. Despite its recent recessionary struggles, the United States economy reigns as the largest and strongest in the world, lending confidence to those who store their value in dollar denominated U.S. Treasuries. Combined with the liquidity of Treasury securities and vast depth of the market (meaning that the market is relatively stable, as its size makes it less subject to the shifts in value that can result when a large amount of a particular security is bought or sold at once), that confidence makes the U.S. dollar quite a safe bet.

What is the benefit of reserve currency status?

As we dig into the benefits of reserve currency status, let's consider what it means to the issuing country. It certainly sounds important. But the advantages of issuing the currency that the world holds in reserve are significant. Perhaps, the most notable benefit, at least from a financial standpoint, is the ability of the issuing country to avoid transaction costs when trading abroad. Since the dollar is the standard, other countries generally must convert their currencies to dollars in order to do business with the United States.

Other currencies such as the euro, the yen, and the yuan, among others, are sometimes accepted and used. But the dollar is universally accepted. For the United States, this eliminates the inherent exchange rate risk that other countries face in converting their currencies to dollars. Further, other countries are motivated to conduct their monetary policies in relation to the United States in an attempt to keep the values of their domestic currencies from straying too far from the dollar. This gives the United States the freedom to make policy decisions from a purely domestic standpoint, where leaders of other countries must operate within their own frameworks while still considering U.S. policy. If their domestic currency weakens in relation to the dollar, they face the prospect of inflation. And if their currency appreciates, they naturally become concerned about their export sector.

An issuer of reserve currency maintains more autonomy in going about its international transactions, enjoying the benefit of doing business in its own currency, with lower transaction costs. Add to that the lower borrowing costs derived as a result of other countries choosing to hold their dollar denominated reserves in the form of U.S. Treasuries. This demand for Treasury bonds encourages stability in the U.S. bond market. Along with that steady foreign demand for the securities comes downward pressure on bond yields, reducing the net cost of borrowing for the United States. While it may not be a direct effect, this is just another benefit of having the dollar accepted in most every country in the world.

Finally, we can also talk about a form of insurance that the United States obtains by having international contracts denominated in U.S. dollars. Suppose the United States owes $1 trillion to the rest of the world. The crucial part of this example is that the American foreign debt is denominated in dollars. At the same time, the United States also owns foreign assets. For the sake of our example, let's assume the United States owns €500 billion worth of euro-denominated bonds. Now suppose the dollar depreciates against the euro—let's say each $1 was trading for €0.85, and then loses value and becomes $1 to €0.75. What happened to the debt that the United States owed to the rest of the world? It began at $1 trillion and stays at $1 trillion. In other words, because the debt is in dollars, its value does not respond to the exchange rate change.

How about the value of American holdings of foreign assets? In dollar terms, the €500 billion worth of euro bonds was worth $588 billion at the $1 to €0.85 exchange rate. When the dollar depreciates and now only trades for €0.75, the value of those same euro bonds rises to $667 billion! So, a depreciating value of the dollar boosts the United States in terms of the value of its foreign assets, while the U.S. liabilities to the rest of the world are mainly unchanged since most or all of U.S. liabilities are in terms of the dollar.

Costs

We cannot examine the benefits of world reserve currency status without asking whether there are costs. Are there drawbacks? And, if so, what are they? Well, as with everything in economics, of course there are two sides to this.

We just explained how the U.S. dollar acting as world reserve currency provides insurance for the United States when the dollar depreciates. Unfortunately, the reverse is true of other countries, who become the recipients of *negative* insurance, so to speak. Let's see this with a numerical example. Suppose the Philippines has $100 million in foreign liabilities that they owe to the rest of the world (for example, they could owe money to Saudi Arabia for oil contracts that are denominated in U.S. dollars), and let's assume that the dollar-peso exchange rate is $1 to ₱50. Therefore, in terms of their own currency, their liabilities are valued at ₱5 billion. Now, the dollar depreciates against all currencies in the world for some reason that has nothing to do with what is happening in the Philippines. Suppose the exchange rate becomes $1 to ₱60. Now, the value of debt that the Philippines owes to the rest of the world just went up to ₱6 billion, even though they did nothing wrong themselves! So, the dollar acting as the world reserve currency can benefit the United States while it simultaneously penalizes the rest of the world.

An additional cost for the United States of having the principal world reserve currency is lower bond yields. When other countries continue to purchase and hold U.S. Treasury securities, it does indeed suppress yields, which leads some to argue that the lower borrowing costs serve as incentive for the government to perpetuate its appetite for deficit spending. And while we could argue the validity of the spending programs and the extent to which the borrowing costs actually influence the rate at which the government chooses to spend, some economists consider this side-effect of reserve currency status to be a drawback.

Another downside of operating as a reserve currency issuer is the resulting continual running of a trade deficit. As other countries are purchasing dollar denominated assets, the United States runs an ongoing trade account deficit, meaning that imports into the United States are outpacing exports to other countries. Is this a bad thing? Well, imports into a rapidly growing economy generally indicate that a country is bringing in resources needed for production, while exports represent goods that have been produced for sale abroad. And the dollars being sent overseas for purchases of imported goods are either held there in reserve or used by those foreign countries to invest in dollar denominated assets. So, while increases in imports can signify production expansion, running a trade deficit for too long might lead to a build-up in foreign investment in U.S. assets. And the income paid to the foreign owners of those investments, whether they are Treasury securities, stocks in American companies, or real estate, would ship even more dollars overseas.

Typically, a country that runs a trade deficit also experiences higher national debt and, therefore, relatively slower growth. The build-up in debt is generally viewed as a drawback of reserve currency status. And, depending on the circumstances, it can be an inhibitor to growth and, therefore, a cost of reserve status. Consider, however, that the United States has been the world's reserve currency issuer for decades and the boom in economic growth that the nation experienced over that time period is astounding. So, while this potential burden of world reserve currency status may be unbearable for some, it has not been an obstacle for the United States.

With its ability to manage economic stress by quickly adapting to changing conditions, the U.S. financial system has proven that it is resilient enough to weather storms. As a case in point, action taken by the U.S. government during the 2008–2009 global financial crisis, through its monetary policies, not only helped to stabilize the American banking system but also is attributed with dampening the recessionary impact to other countries. If the dollar's value had fallen drastically, the impact to the rest of the world could have been much greater.

Although there are those who worry that the net exporting of dollars may eventually erode the strength of the currency, we must not lose sight of the fact that the dollar has maintained its status as the standard for the world since the 1920s. The world has confidence in the dollar as a store of value and in U.S. policymakers. This optimism and confidence make the dollar uniquely suited to be the world reserve currency.

The rise of the dollar

So, how did the dollar attain its status as the world reserve currency? Well, it evolved naturally as the United States gained prominence in the world marketplace. In ancient times, the dominant currencies shifted as different countries emerged as leaders of regional commerce. The British pound began a long reign as the reserve of choice in the 1800s, as Great Britain became the world's largest manufacturer, leading in the exports of finished goods and imports of raw materials.

At that time, most countries had begun to store gold in reserve. With the British pound being used for international trade and easily convertible into gold, its evolution as the world reserve currency was obvious. Moving into the 1900s, European countries such as France and Germany became larger players in international trade and their currencies became more prevalent, shifting prominence away from the British pound. Generally speaking, the period from 1915 to 1930 (the World War I era), brought about the end of the pound's reign as world reserve currency. The transition was accelerated by the 1944 Bretton Woods Agreement, whereupon the U.S. dollar became the official world reserve currency (until the Bretton Woods Agreement was abandoned in 1973), and it was solidified in the aftermath of World War II.

By the end of the war in 1945, most of the developed world, particularly Europe and Japan, lay physically decimated. The United States, on the other hand, had not suffered the destruction of battle on its mainland. Though the American economy had been converted from domestic production to war-time manufacturing (from cars to bombers), the country's industrial facilities and infrastructure were still intact. Companies simply pushed aside the tooling for guns and war planes and pulled back the equipment side-lined in 1942, making a speedy return to domestic production. War-torn countries faced a very different path to return to normal production levels.

In full production mode, armed with the newest technologies learned during wartime manufacturing, the United States became an industrial behemoth with relatively greater prominence within the world than ever before. Rapidly growing productivity allowed the nation to become a huge importer of goods. This demand for foreign goods and materials helped fuel the rebound for other countries' domestic economies. And as these foreign countries recovered and began exporting goods to the United States, they were importing the dollars used as payment for these goods.

Those dollars were no more than demand notes, backed by the U.S. government, to be used by these countries in the future. Would these dollars hold their face value over time? Could those dollar holding countries redeem them for goods in the future? What was it about U.S. dollars that gave foreign holders the confidence to accept all this paper? Well, the Bretton Woods Agreement had established an international monetary system that fixed exchange rates to the U.S. dollar and anchored currencies to gold. So, yes, the dollars operated under a *gold exchange standard (a hybrid of the traditional gold standard and a reserve currency system)*, meaning that a holder could, under that system, return the dollars to the United States and redeem them for gold, although some economists pointed out that the United States would never be able to actually redeem all of the outstanding dollars for gold, which built an inherent confidence problem into the Bretton Woods system. But was the Bretton Woods Agreement alone enough to elevate the dollar to international reserve status?

The simple answer, of course, is no. The reason that other countries were, and arguably still are, happy to hold dollars as reserves against their own currency is that the dollars represented stable purchasing power. The view of the United States as a strong, secure nation in the aftermath of World War II carried over to the dollar, lending confidence in its value and stability. So, while it had already become an international means of transacting business, the worldwide acceptance of the dollar was solidified by the post-World War II boom, catapulting it into world reserve status.

Will the dollar fall?

Will the dollar continue to reign supreme? This question is often the focus of news stories. To understand the variables involved, let's take a look at the factors that typically distinguish a world reserve currency.

- *Availability*: There must be a significant amount of that currency in circulation around the globe, growing in quantity to meet demand. If it is to be held in reserve internationally, there must be enough of the currency to satisfy the demand of the other countries that will hold it. It is simple supply and demand, really.
- *Growth*: The currency must generally be growing faster than others, which logically means that the country's GDP must be growing at a relatively faster rate.
- *Stability*: The currency must be highly liquid and stable. While foreign countries hold sizable stores of reserves in cash, many choose to hold income producing securities denominated in the reserve currency. But they must have confidence that the securities may be quickly converted into cash and that they will hold their value in a crisis. Market depth is important in maintaining stability because it prevents ripples in value when larger lots of the security are purchased or sold. U.S. Treasury securities, in addition to being highly convertible, are viewed as one of the safest, most stable assets on the market.
- *Trade Deficit*: The country issuing the currency must export significant amounts of the currency in exchange for imported goods and services. In other words, a country whose currency operates as a world reserve is typically a net importer, running a trade deficit with the other large economies in the world.

That last bit about a trade deficit sounds worrisome because classic economics teaches us that an economy can only grow if it is a net exporter. And, indeed, when the United States was growing at the rate that established it as the world reserve currency, it often did lead the world in exports. But the flip side of the trade deficit is the financial account surplus. Our record of international accounts with the rest of the world is known as the Balance of Payments, which is made up of the current account, the financial account, and the capital account. Just like our accounting rules mandate, these must all sum up to zero.

While a deficit is generally considered to be a bad thing, there are both good and bad points in this case. We have pointed out that other countries are accumulating stores of dollars, and those dollars enable them to purchase our exports. And, while they also use the dollars to invest in American assets, remember that, since the dollar is the world reserve, other countries want to *hold* dollars or Treasury securities. That means they are not motivated to cash out their securities or exchange the currency for goods and services. So, the U.S. economy has actually seen a net benefit of the trade deficit, as the inflow of goods and services from abroad has helped to boost standards of living. And we have financed it to a great extent with credit, whether in the form of demand notes (i.e. cash) sitting in foreign banks or Treasury securities.

So, let's return to our question. Is the dollar at risk to lose its status and strength as the world's reserve currency? The economic conditions in the United States during the Great Recession of 2008–2009 naturally bring worries to the forefront. Many economists argue that the euro may become the primary reserve currency. It is widely accepted in settlement of international trade, with the size of the Eurozone's economy supporting its rise. Others believe that China's rapidly growing economy will bring the yuan to the forefront. Despite the PBOC's strict control, the yuan's standing in the world is gaining acceptance and popularity, making it a world player.

There are several dominant reserve currencies, all held with respect and confidence. Rather than overtake the dollar, these currencies operate alongside it as a means of international exchange. While it is true that these currencies are held in a *reserve basket* of sorts, it is unlikely that any other currency will replace the dollar, at least in the foreseeable future.

So, we must remember that there is a difference in a currency being used to settle international payments and actually being held *in reserve*. As things currently stand, financial markets and global firms and citizens look to the dollar and U.S. policymakers when the global economy faces any sort of uncertainty, and this seems unlikely to change any time soon.

What about the euro?

The euro, as we know, is the currency used by the 19 Eurozone countries. While it does comprise a significant trading zone, the Eurozone does not present as a united front in other financial and political aspects. As previously mentioned, while the Eurozone's monetary policy is unified by the common currency and common central bank, its fiscal policy coordination is lacking, while it is even debatable whether the Eurozone is even an optimum currency area at all. Think about strong Germany and weak Greece, in this era.

And while the member countries are some of the world's oldest, the Euro-zone is quite young. Reserve currency status is generally attained by mature economies with some type of track record. So, will other countries choose the Euro over the dollar? It does not appear to be on the horizon in the near future.

The Chinese Yuan/Renminbi

China, with its rising emergence as an economic powerhouse, is still a cen-trally planned country, with its central bank (PBOC) run by major political leaders. The PBOC is strong, and rich in assets, yet the private sector has much more room for growth. In particular, many Chinese citizens cannot afford to purchase large quantities of goods from abroad. Add to that the fact that the Chinese government maintains tight restrictions on the types of assets its citizens are permitted to hold (capital controls), only allowing them very small amounts of foreign currency. Let's not forget that China has long maintained its position as a net exporter. In fact, China frequently holds a large a huge trade surplus with the United States, amassing a vast amount of dollars in reserve.

So, would they alter course, suddenly deciding to let its currency appre-ciate to market rates, enabling its citizens to trade abroad and gobble up imports and thereby becoming a net exporter of yuan? History does not pro-vide any indication of this desire. If other countries are not exporting large amounts of goods to China, those countries will have no way of obtaining yuan to hold in reserve. So, while China is without a doubt an economic superpower, it's current and recent policies make the yuan unlikely to take the status of the world reserve currency in the next several years.

The U.S. economy has inspired confidence among trading partners world-wide for many decades now, and since one of the primary components of world reserve currency status is confidence in the currency's liquidity and stability, there is little reason to suspect this will change any time soon.

Key terms

- **Reserve Currency**—a currency that is held in large quantities by other central banks of the world as a part of their holdings of foreign exchange reserves.
- **Trade Deficit**—the situation where a country's value of imports exceeds its value of exports.
- **Reserve Currency System**—an international monetary system where countries fix their exchange rate against the reserve country's currency.
- **Gold Standard**—a global system where countries fix their currency val-ues to the price of gold.
- **Bretton Woods Agreement**—a collective global foreign exchange regime that lasted from 1945 to 1973, where countries pegged their currency

values to the U.S. dollar, who in turn fixed the dollar to gold. This was *a gold exchange standard*, which is a hybrid of the reserve currency system and a gold standard.

• **Balance of Payments**—the account that records all international transactions between one country and the rest of the world over a given period of time.

End-of-chapter problems

1. Considering reserve currencies in history:

    a. What historical system made the U.S. dollar the reserve currency of the world?

    b. Name two or three reasons why we departed from this system.

2. Doing some online research of your own, define:

    a. What does it mean for a currency to be 'convertible?'

    b. What is a 'vehicle' currency?

    c. Using your answers to (a) and (b), can you list some reasons why the U.S. dollar has remained the primary world reserve currency?

3. If a country has reserve currency status, does it need to be concerned with foreign exchange rate risk? If not, why do these countries still frequently use forward or futures contracts for currencies?

4. Consider an advanced country (U.S.) and a developing country (Malaysia):

    a. Suppose that the demand for Malaysia exports increases. What do you expect to happen to the Malaysian Ringitt (RM)-U.S. dollar exchange rate? Explain your answer briefly.

    b. If U.S. foreign liabilities are denominated entirely in U.S. dollars, do debt obligations from the United States to the rest of the world rise, fall, or stay the same? Explain your answer briefly.

    c. If the United States holds Malaysian government bonds in their portfolio of assets, what happens to the dollar value of these particular foreign holdings? Explain your answer briefly.

    d. If Malaysia's foreign liabilities are denominated entirely in U.S. dollars, does Malaysia's net foreign debt (in Ringitt) rise, fall, or stay the same? Explain your answer briefly.

5. From national income accounting, a trade deficit is equal to the difference between savings and investment for a country, which means a larger deficit can finance more investment. Can this be a good reason for a country to justify running a trade deficit?

6. Discuss whether the euro could ever become the world reserve currency according to the criteria of availability, growth, stability, and trade balance.

7. Repeat the previous question's analysis, but for the Chinese Yuan this time.

8. If you could build a basket of currencies to jointly act as the reserve currencies of the world, which two currencies would you include besides the U.S. dollar, the euro, and the Chinese Yuan, and why?

Part II

Related topics

With so many varying opinions proffered, deciphering current economics can be a bit like the proverbial quandary of being unable to 'see the forest for the trees.' A well-written article or essay can leave us with a sense that we should rely on what the author is saying because they have presented it in such a neatly wrapped package. And while that may be true with some topics, economics is one of those areas where well versed opinions can easily be mistaken for fact. There are so many moving parts in an economy that, even with a good dose of basic understanding, it can be a daunting task to try to figure out what works and what doesn't, especially when taking a micro idea and extrapolating its impact on a macro level. In fact, notable, well-educated economic 'experts' often disagree. It makes for good press but it can also cloud the issue for the reader who just wants to understand how things that affect their daily life are expected to change. If you sift through all of the clutter, it becomes clear that if you can grasp basic accounting principles and use a little common sense, you can generally step back from the 'trees' and see the 'forest' for what it is. That was the inspiration of the first part of this book. The most powerful tool we can strive for is knowledge and by improving our understanding of economics as applied to our daily lives, we can make better decisions for ourselves and those around us.

As we touched on in each of the previous sections, confidence is perhaps the most important factor in a healthy economy. In Chapter 1, we looked at three pillars; confidence, monetary policy and fiscal policy. Monetary and fiscal policy matters are often the subject of news stories and political debates. But confidence is seldom a topic of discussion. While we must have sound policies in place, confidence is the key to a robust and thriving economy. When the future is perceived to be solid, the economy moves forward with enthusiasm. A lack of confidence translates into fear for the future. Businesses and consumers pull back, leading to stagnation and, if it continues long enough, recession. Although it attracts little attention, the impact of confidence is pervasive. So, as we move into the second part of this book, we must keep in mind that, while political and other considerations may come into play when focusing on a particular sector of the economy, confidence remains as the critical element for stability and growth.

DOI: 10.4324/9781003251453-11

Now that we have covered the framework for understanding economics, we can take a look at some specific topics that affect each of us on a daily basis. After all, the point of it goes beyond being able to make sense of the news. Ideally, we will be able to use the understanding of how things work in our world to anticipate the future and implement strategies. Simply put, we can become proactive instead of reactive. To that end, we are going to take a deeper look at four specific areas. Each of us can identify in some fashion with real estate values, oil prices, and the fluctuating value of gold. Unlike stocks and bonds, these three areas in particular represent things that almost everyone will deal with at some point in their lives. Even the most cash oriented person who will never purchase a single share of stock will probably buy gas for their car. They will live somewhere, either renting or owning a home, so the value of that property will hold significance in their financial life. And they might wear or give a piece of jewelry to a loved one. You may wonder why these three were chosen for discussion. Well, in addition to being commonplace in our daily lives, each of them is unique in some way regarding value. And, while easily identifiable by the average person, each of them is often misunderstood in terms of economics, giving them particular interest for inclusion in this book.

In addition to these three topics, we will also consider a growing trend in modern finance, namely cryptocurrencies. We will present what they are, how they have functioned, and what may lay in store for the future.

9 Real estate

Objectives

1. To understand how real estate is valued.
2. We will examine what factors, such as demographics, cause the value of real estate to change over time.
3. We will also consider real estate from the perspective of investment, including a brief description of a few tax considerations.

By its very nature, real estate is different from any other kind of investment. No other physical or financial asset behaves quite like real property. The total value of all real estate in the U.S. is estimated to be worth over 36 trillion dollars as of 2020, which was almost two times our annual GDP. Real estate represents perhaps 20% of the value of all assets in the U.S., making it critical to understand its role in the overall economy as well as our individual economic lives.

Whether it is our personal home or business property, it is the largest asset in value that most people own. We form emotional attachments to real estate as a result of life experiences and memories that are connected to particular buildings or land, making it sometimes difficult to separate that connection in order to take an objective approach to buying and selling property. And because we all live, work and play in or on real estate every day, we have a sense of understanding about it that is not necessarily characteristic of other investment categories.

But do we really understand the impact of real estate values in the ups and downs of the economy? Of all of the lost value in various asset categories during the 2008–2009 Great Recession, real estate suffered perhaps the most severely, with far-reaching impacts on the lives of many people. So, our focus for discussion is aimed at gaining a better understanding of how real estate is valued, how its value changes over time, and how to think about it from a purely investment standpoint.

Valuing a real property investment

For the average citizen, real estate ownership means purchasing a home. Most of us will never become investors in commercial property. However,

DOI: 10.4324/9781003251453-12

when we think of the way property is valued, investment becomes an important concept. Because the guidelines for determining the fair market value of an investment property are based on objective measures, they can also be helpful when entering the market for a home. The basic skills that investors use will certainly benefit a buyer who is attempting to balance the needs of his or her family with budgetary constraints. And even if one's budget is not the primary focus, learning to think like an investor certainly cannot hurt when purchasing a home.

Valuation methodology as applied to income producing real estate is well understood by most real estate investors. The predominant method used to determine value for this type of property, the Income Capitalization Approach, begins with one simple question: how much rent will it produce? Of course, an investor will want to look at other elements such as the condition of the property, any anticipated extraordinary costs, possible zoning or regulatory changes and other concerns that could impact the current or future value of the property. As with any investment, income and appreciation may be the two most important factors, but particularly with real estate, the starting point is typically its annual cash flow.

It should be noted that there are a number of methodologies available for property valuation. Capitalization of Income is one of several methods used by valuation professionals and sophisticated investors. While others, such as Discounted Cash Flows, are sometimes used, the Capitalization of Income approach is the most common. Primarily due to its fundamental premise, which extrapolates a future market value from current operating income, it seems particularly well suited for valuing investment real estate.

Other methods are based on different lines of thought. The Discounted Cash Flows method, for example, is calculated by developing projected cash flow data and then discounting the future expected operating income back to the present to determine current value; think back to our discussion of bond prices in an earlier chapter, where we formally saw how one can discount a future stream of income. If you are reviewing a report from a professional appraiser, note the method he or she used to determine and compare values. That will help you understand the thought process behind the results as well as determine the amount of weight you place upon the appraised value in making your own analysis.

If an investor is scouting for properties to purchase and hold, their starting point should be the *net operating income* or *NOI*. Basically, they want to know how much cash flow will remain after payment of all annual operating expenses, but before debt service, capital improvements or income taxes.

For example, imagine that a commercial office building is for sale, which is listed at $500,000. The potential investor, in doing their due diligence, learns that the property produces annual gross rents of $100,000. In order to determine net operating income, the investor must convert this gross income to the amount left over after the expenses of operation are paid. If these expenses are $40,000 (property taxes, insurance, repairs, accounting costs, leasing costs, etc.), then the NOI is $60,000.

This is a handy benchmark, but it should be noted that NOI, as used in property valuation, would most likely begin with *normalized income*, which would adjust for any unusual variances in the gross rental income as well as factoring in an adjustment for expected vacancies. Expenses would be normalized as well, adjusting for one-time payments or changes in the allocation of expenses between the landlord and tenant. For example, negotiations with a new tenant may result in the tenant assuming payment of the property taxes. So, if we determine that the $100,000 gross rental income is a good average and normalized expenses will be about $60,000, the resulting annual NOI is $40,000.

While the NOI for a particular property is quite useful as a quick method for an investor to measure performance, it does not tell the investor what he should expect to pay for the property. That is where the valuation comes in. Using the capitalization of income method, the NOI of $40,000 will be used with a *capitalization rate*, or *cap rate*, to develop a market sales price for this property. The cap rate is determined by the following formula:

$$\text{Cap Rate} = \frac{\text{Annual Operating Income (NOI)}}{\text{Value of Property (Cost)}}$$

In this example:

$$\text{Cap Rate} = \frac{\$40,000 \text{ (NOI)}}{\$500,000 \text{ (Price of Building)}} = 8\%$$

The cap rate is a handy tool for a potential investor to use in scouting the market. It gives potential investors a number for their return on investment, which can then be compared to alternative expected returns. For example, an investor would not buy this commercial building with a cap rate of 8% if their regular savings account offered an interest rate of 10%. The cap rate is often used as a rule of thumb and can be particularly useful in spotting trends in a particular market category. For example, if apartment buildings are trading at around an 8% cap rate in the local market, an investor would be able to use the NOI of a potential investment to determine whether they should purchase this property. If the market cap rate suddenly begins dropping, the property becomes less attractive to the investor. The investor may also wonder if a bubble in the apartment building market is forming, which has driven up property values.

As useful as the cap rate is, however, it can be misleading if a user does not clearly understand its purpose and limitations. While it does provide a quick look at the potential for a property, it is not all-inclusive. It is simply a quick way to explain the relationship between NOI and market asking price and it is useful in spotting trends in a particular market category. Cap rate analysis is limited in that it provides a snapshot of the investment that can change at any time. And it is only as reliable as the data used to make the calculation. While it can be a remarkably accurate predictor of expected cash flow, especially when normalized data is used, an investor should consider whether a more in-depth analysis of the property's condition and cash flows might be in order.

The investor should consider all aspects of the investment, not just the picture painted by the net operating income. After all, they should be looking toward future returns and the potential for appreciation. The NOI could change based on any number of factors. So, even if a property passes the cap rate test, many other facts should be considered:

- Market saturation in the area (supply and demand imbalance)
- Age of the building (are major repairs needed?)
- Economic outlook for the local area
- Economic outlook for the nation
- Other investment opportunities (both real estate and other)
- Local demographics and anticipated growth
- Credit worthiness of current or expected future tenants
- Other factors specific to the property or area, such as new highways or business development underway or potential for highway traffic to bypass the area with new roads being planned.

Any of the above factors could significantly impact the market value of a property. So, in this example, is a $500,000 asking price reasonable for a building which currently produces an annual NOI of $40,000? Well, maybe. If we assume that all other factors listed above are perceived to have been satisfactorily met in the potential investor's analysis, what else is left for consideration?

Financing considerations

One big factor in determining the overall return on an investment, maybe the most important of all, is the interest rate. While it is easy to become caught up in the analysis of an investment property from a net operating income or cap rate point of view, an investor should not forget about net cash return. Unless it is a cash purchase, the investment will be financed. So, an investor must factor in the potential cost of borrowing as part of their overall picture, asking themselves some important questions, including the following:

- What return will I receive from this building?
- How much down payment can I afford?
- How much bank financing will I need and at what rate?
- Will I need to refinance in the future?

- What are the lending terms that I must meet, such as loan-to-value ratio and personal net worth?
- What are the remaining terms of any current tenants' leases and how do they compare to others in the area?
- What can I expect the market to support when those tenants renew, or the space is released?

A prudent investor will take a step back and investigate a potential investment objectively, including all aspects of the property that may affect overall return.

By the way, note that the NOI and cap rate are crucial even when the purchase is done fully with cash. For example, if you estimate the cap rate at 5%, and you expect a return on bonds or on your stock holdings of 6%, with other things equal, you would not purchase the property, even if you did not need a loan to finance the purchase.

Tax considerations

While most investors are not tax experts, and do not aspire to be, it is helpful to understand a few simple concepts related to real estate investments. While income tax expense is not considered in determining market value for a particular property, taxes do impact net profit. As such, income tax considerations may be a significant factor in an investor's analysis of a property. This is certainly not an all-inclusive list of tax concerns, nor is it meant to be. Each taxpayer's situation is different, making it impossible to determine the way that a particular tax provision will impact his or her return without reviewing the specific facts. For investors, it is best to have some general knowledge of the concepts but leave the more complex matters to a professional.

When it comes to rental real estate, probably the most often mentioned tax deduction is depreciation. This is a broad concept but, in general terms, it relates to the fact that property will age over time, with the value of the property decreasing in some respects as a result of that aging process. In recognition of this reduction in value, the cost of a building or a component of that building, furnishings or any improvements is generally subject to depreciation rules. Basically, that means that the cost of those items is not deducted for tax purposes in the year of acquisition. Instead, deductions are spread over a specified number of years and those annual deductions are taken against the income generated by the property. So, although it is not an expense actually paid in the year to which it applies, it is a deduction on that year's tax return. While the actual calculations are probably best left to a tax professional, an investor should understand that certain expenses may not be fully deductible in the year in which they are paid, but instead taken as installments over some period of years.

For real estate investors, there are two types of tax with regard to rental properties. First of all, the net taxable income from operating rental property is generally subject to income tax at ordinary tax rates. While there are some detailed and complicated rules involved, this typically means that the income is reportable and taxable similarly to wages and other forms of compensation. The other type of tax that investors should be aware of is capital gains tax. This is the tax applicable to any gain realized on properties when they are sold. It is generally levied at a lower rate than the tax on ordinary income, making it a bit less painful for investors.

In the United States, the tax code imposes different tax treatment for certain activities. For rental property owners, the passive activity rules can be particularly problematic. The rules, which apply to most rental real estate owners who are not actively managing the property on a daily basis, are quite complex. Essentially, they provide that passive investors can only deduct losses from operation of a property to the extent that there gains from that property. Because of the complexity of these rules, most rental property owners find that it is well worth the cost of hiring a tax professional for navigation of the passive activity rules, as well as general tax preparation and planning.

The perfect storm

If you read mainstream news publications, you'll see that many journalists have come to believe that rampant demand and the expanding money supply (M2) in the economy were the big factors in pushing real estate values to unsustainable highs in the early-to-mid-2000s. The theory goes that the housing boom was largely a function of the Federal Reserve providing so much liquidity to the commercial banking system that real estate values had to respond. However, if you understand the fundamentals of the modern banking system, you know that this is an overly simplistic story.

The Fed's policies certainly played a role in the housing bubble. A low Fed funds rate permitted banks to lower interest rates on mortgage loans, reducing the cost of borrowing. This made mortgages more affordable and brought more borrowers to the table, which worked in concert with other market conditions to increase demand. Rising demand pushed up appraisal values and provided seemingly reliable collateral for loans. The market was bustling and lenders began competing for business, advertising low mortgage rates and simplified paperwork. But the availability of lending alone cannot drive buyers into the market. Demand is not driven purely by availability of funds. Rather, there must be confidence in the economy and a belief that values will rise. So, while the banking system facilitated the situation, there were other factors at play. Let's take a look at the dynamics of the crisis.

At the center of what was really a perfect storm was an unprecedented boom in real estate values. The early-to-mid-2000s saw home prices skyrocket with double digit growth in many areas. If you look at longer term historical trends for housing prices, you will see a pattern of growth, but it is obvious that this spike was far from the norm. Why did this happen?

We know that credit policies were significantly relaxed, partly in response to government legislation pertaining to housing, and partly due to competition for profits that skewed the risk vs. reward models for some lenders. Then came the subprime mortgage packages that we've heard so much about: borrowers with less than stellar credit were suddenly able to easily obtain mortgages, often with little documentation of assets or verification of income. This then raised demand, which, in turn, put upward pressure on prices.

There have always been mortgage products for those with impaired credit. The subprime mortgage was not new in the early 2000s. But the prolific use of it was a new phenomenon. Typically, subprime borrowers would be subject to higher interest rates, larger down payments and other loan features that would be characteristic of higher risk mortgages. And some of the borrowing that took place during the bubble did include some risk-adjustment factors, but it was typically less than prudent, leaving lenders with precarious exposure to risk. And it was all based on inflated real estate values.

Adding fuel to the growing fire was the more commonplace view toward home ownership as a right, not a privilege. No one would fault those who were attempting to better their lives—yet it should only be done in a responsible and financially sound way. The fault lies also with lenders who failed in doing their due diligence. In an effort to garner higher profits, they lowered their standards and began to compete more aggressively for customers.

In their defense, U.S. government agencies seemed to support this position, with Fannie Mae and others continuing to promote the vigorous lending activity. Further, although it appears quite reckless in hindsight, the financial industry was responding rationally to the conditions in the market. When the economy took a downturn in the early 2000s, following the September 11, 2001 terrorist attacks and the fallout of the *dotcom bubble*, the Fed funds rate dropped to a record low of 1%. This kept lending, specifically in the housing market, relatively stable while other segments of the economy were suffering. As is typical when the stock market is in turmoil, investors fled to the safety of Treasury bonds. Bond yields were pushed down, providing less return for holders, so banks and investment firms began seeking opportunities for greater returns.

Typically, as we know, the risk that a particular investment offers rises along with the potential return. This situation was no different. With cheap money available, the demand for the larger returns provided by riskier investment vehicles increased. Financial firms responded by securitizing subprime mortgages, resulting in the market frenzy driven by the now infamous mortgage-backed securities, which ultimately became illiquid, as they were difficult to unwind, further depressing their values. In hindsight, we can see that the banks and financial firms were responding to investors' demand for return and increased appetite for risk. So, while it is tempting to blame the bankers, we must step back and understand that, even though they were acting less than prudently, they did so in response to market pressures and governmental policies. Yes, it ended badly. But it was not sinister intent, but market demand and loose lending policies that set the stage for the fall.

When you combine growing demand and ease of borrowing, you see a spike in the housing market that grabs the attention of many hopeful investors. Along with the suggestion that home ownership is a right comes the idea that housing is also an investment. And when you consider that most people view real estate as a more stable asset than the stock market, you can see how speculators tuned right into what they saw as a ripe opportunity. New investors were coming to the table in droves as they bet on what they believed would be fast appreciation on a high-demand asset. Soon, there was almost a frenzy as rental property ownership and *house flipping* became more commonplace than ever before. And all of this activity was fueled by easier borrowing, which in turn helped create more demand, which led to higher prices. It is easy, then, to see how the cycle continued with very little consideration being given to the precarious nature of the entire build-up. Hence, the very fitting term *bubble*.

We all know what happened next. In 2007, the bubble burst and the fallout was devastating to the real estate industry. Most believed that it was a housing crisis created by the sudden decline in values. Really, it was the end of what was an unsustainable rate of appreciation which was followed by panic that caused that appreciation to turn negative. But that downturn would have had a much less widespread impact without the massive growth in debt that had fed the bubble. The panic was justified, in that loan to value ratios were higher than ever before, meaning that even small drops in collateral value would cause real concern. And with higher aggregate household debt levels than ever before, the impact of the fallout was much more widespread than it might otherwise have been.

The effects of the credit crisis were far-reaching, and no industry was considered safe. Almost everyone was affected by the recession. Unemployment spiked and those who were employed became fearful of being laid off. Many were faced with wage reductions and discretionary spending came to a screeching halt. Confidence in the economy faltered, contracting demand. Unemployment was on the rise and GDP began to stall. As incomes dropped, borrowers began to fall behind on loan payments. Now *upside down* due to home values that had fallen below outstanding loan principal balances, many loans went into default.

Banks, under pressure to meet capital ratio requirements in the face of falling loan portfolio and collateral values, began calling loans en masse. Often evaluating credit worthiness of borrowers and calling even loans that were considered current, banks became the bad guys in the eyes of many frightened investors. This fallout was reported as a failure of the government to regulate the banks and it was often misunderstood by the media and the public. But at the end of the day, it was a deleveraging process that resulted in perhaps the worst economic conditions many can remember. There were more sellers than buyers in the market and values entered a downward spiral. We can see the behavior of house prices during the Great

Recession in Figure 9.1 which shows the median sales price of houses sold in the United States.

What went up came back down: the figure shows the sharp fall in prices from early 2007 until the latter half of 2009 (roughly a 20% drop). Harkening back to the Great Depression, which many of us immediately think of when talking about economic disasters, what was initially termed a *balance sheet recession* has now become known as The Great Recession.

When it became evident that the banking system was caught in a credit crisis of epic proportions, emergency intervention became unavoidable. While many were opposed to bailing out the banks, the alternative was to allow the banking system to fail. Although some banks may have weathered the storm, anyone who understands the banking system knows that it is a network of independent banks working in concert as the engine of the economy. Allowing portions of the network to collapse would have pushed the faltering economy further over the edge. By choosing to intervene, the Federal Reserve propped up the banks' reserve accounts and helped stabilize their capital. It was not an effort to push money into the economy, as many believed, but an attempt to restore stability and help ease the fear that had begun to permeate the entire economy.

In lending to banks and purchasing bad assets, the Federal Reserve's intention was to prevent bank failures, reduce stress from weak capital positions, strengthen liquidity, and improve overall balance sheet health. The

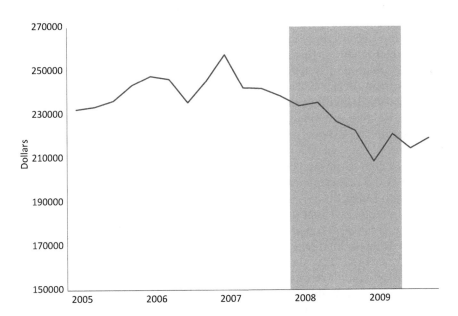

Figure 9.1 Median Sales Price of Houses Sold in the United States.
Source: Census; HUD

result, however, was far more widespread. With some perspective, we can now see that the end result of the Fed's action was to restore confidence in the banking system as a whole, and thereby, begin to plant the seeds of recovery.

Learning from the past

While the recession of the 2000s is simple enough to look at in hindsight as just a bubble that burst, there were many other factors that came into play besides increases in demand and loose lending policies. Demand didn't just suddenly begin to grow in 2000. The spike that occurred was predated by a gradual build-up in demand that naturally occurred along with demographic and cultural changes that were soon reflected in investment portfolios.

In the United States, as people came to view housing as an investment, the brokerage industry responded. Prior to the early 1980s, the real estate market was not liquid. Each investment property was typically owned by a small group of investors or by an individual. Because it was more cumbersome, time consuming, and costly (i.e., more transaction costs) to buy and sell properties this way, real estate was, as a category, less valuable than other forms of investment. Further, the risk of owning properties with limited liability protection made the endeavor less attractive for small investors. Cap rates in the 1970s hovered in the 10%–12% range.

By the early 1980s, however, a popular real estate ownership structure called a limited partnership came into widespread usage. To simplify purchases and address risk exposure, a general partnership would be formed to own a small percentage of a property and manage it, with multiple limited partners providing equity financing in exchange for ownership interests. Although the limited partners had less input in the management of the property, the potential income and appreciation over time provided motivation for investment. Because of the ease of entry and lower transaction costs for the typical small investor, the appeal of real estate as a category grew, bringing new investors and much money into the real estate sector. With this new supply of dollars driving new demand, values of real property rose across the board.

This, of course, pushed cap rates down to a range close to 8%–10%, and ushered in the real estate investment trust or REIT. Although REITs were passed into law in the 1960s in the U.S. during the Eisenhower administration, the unique ownership structure began to gain much more popularity over time as tax laws and other changes combined to make them a desirable entity in which to hold real estate. By the 1990s, they were not only to some extent tax-favored, they were being traded as shares on a somewhat more open market, similar to mutual funds or the stock market. All of this made real estate more valuable in general, lowering cap rates even further to the 5%–7% range by the mid-2000s, setting the stage for the bubble which few saw coming.

Now, very little of the previous discussion of the housing bubble addressed cap rates. And while they wouldn't be a concern for home buyers, investors should have been evaluating potential purchases with some kind of analysis and they most likely considered cap rates. If they did, they would have seen those rates dropping, which could have led to a belief that property values would continue to rise. This belief would have fueled confidence in the real estate market relative to other opportunities, prompting investors to purchase, driving prices higher and higher. And if we take it a step further and look at the net return on the investment, the low interest rates in place, thanks to monetary policy, would entice even the savviest investor. So, while we need to understand cap rates, we need to know how to use them in conjunction with other tools for analysis. We must remember that they are not all inclusive. Common sense and a general understanding of the economy can be as valuable as any rule of thumb or investment tool.

Back to the future

In the earlier example of an 8% cap rate, $40,000 NOI, and $500,000 value for the building, we were saying that an 8% cap rate is a reasonable return for that property in that current interest rate environment. If banks were lending at a rate of 5%, for example, then an owner could enjoy a 3% profit on the difference in the cap rate (8%) and the cost of financing (5%), often called *the spread*, plus anticipated appreciation of the property over time. Assuming the investor is satisfied with all aspects of the property and it meets or exceeds their requirements, this may seem like a good investment. But, what if the NOI is slightly inflated? What if significant expenses were overlooked? Certainly, the cap rate would change. And if the investor is using that as the primary tool to make their investment decision, they might face a very different outcome than expected.

Based on what we know from the Great Recession, what should a buyer consider in addition to cap rates? Unless they know that the market is stable or that this particular property is exceptionally well priced, they might take a step back and look at the overall real estate environment. Is there a possibility of a bubble? Is the lending agency sound? Could the investor withstand the possibility of a change in their lending package, such as having the loan called if the value of the property drops in the future? With the Great Recession in our recent memory, we should take some lessons from it and apply them in such a way as to become wiser investors. There will always be surprises but we can use the new understanding gained from the painful experiences of the past to frame our perspective on new investments in such a way to mitigate risk as well as maximize returns.

Thus, when considering real estate investments, as we know, there are more variables involved than just cap rates. So, a prudent beginning investor will want to compare the potential investment properties to a standard. Remember that the cap rate does not factor in the cost of financing. So, it is really an indicator of the expected return on a cash investment.

Let's assume that we have a fixed sum to invest. Returning to our previous example, assume that we are looking for a way to invest $500,000. Treasury securities are often viewed as a standard for safe investments, making the Treasury bond rate a safe benchmark which is commonly employed when valuing other asset categories, including real estate. If we assume, for purposes of our example, that the current 20-year Treasury Bond rate is around 3.3%, we can use that as a reference point in our cap rate analysis. Since our example produced a cap rate of 8%, we can subtract the 3.3% risk-free Treasury rate from the 8%, resulting in a 4.7% risk premium. Then, when we look at the other underlying fundamentals of the property in question, we can decide if the investment justifies the additional 4.7% risk. Thinking about it in this way sometimes makes it easier to step back and view potential investments in a more objective manner.

The market must take many variables into account in looking toward the future for real estate values. Land and buildings only have value if people have a desire and need for them. That brings into the equation *demographics*, which turns our thinking to the population in the country as well as trends in housing and real estate development. How many people? How much do they earn? Where do they want to live? These factors, of course, drive real estate prices.

Demographers know that an important economic indicator is the *replacement rate*. Strongly tied to the fertility rate, the replacement rate is the number of individuals that must be born to replace those who die. About 2.1 is considered to be the replacement rate necessary to maintain a stable U.S. population. Everyone dies, some sooner than others, but not everyone reproduces. For each generation to replace itself, each female must bear roughly 2.1 children in order to replace herself and her partner and to account for those who either do not survive to childbearing age or who do not reproduce.

In 2020, the actual fertility rate was about 1.6, reflecting a lower birth rate during harsh economic times. Was the drop due only to economic pressures? Probably not, although recent history indicates that the replacement rate may decrease when confidence in the economic future falters. Does it automatically signify a diminishing U.S. population for the future? It doesn't if rapid immigration makes up the difference. The U.S. Census Bureau estimates by 2050 the U.S. will have a population of about 400 million people, up from around 300 million in 2010. More people need more developed real estate on which to live, work, and play.

Prior to the 2020 Covid-19 pandemic, housing market trends favored strong growth in urban areas. Job markets are changing, and more people now work from home or in virtual offices where they telecommute and teleconference. This has opened up opportunities for young, tech-savvy people to choose where they live, and they seem drawn together by the social and cultural opportunities offered in urban settings. And that sense of community is a demographic indicator that many real estate investors are watching. Patterns prior to 2020 indicated a return to urban lifestyles with the term *new urbanism* often heard in context of mixed-use development and the concept of *live, work, play* communities. This could certainly inspire a shift in demand and changes in value as interest in suburban living wanes and young people gravitate toward cities and towns. Yet the pandemic of 2020 has made us question whether cities will remain the places that attract young workers to live and work.

While housing trends led by the younger generations are certainly important, we must also consider our senior population. People are living longer and, therefore, the housing choices of the older class demand attention. A pre-Covid-19 trend indicated that seniors were increasingly opting to relocate to urban communities. Driven by a desire for a low maintenance lifestyle, convenient access to necessary amenities such as grocery and drug stores, as well as proximity to medical care, retirees were starting to leave the suburbs. Senior housing communities have popped up, indicating that the market is responding to the needs of the older segment of the population. We will see how these trends continue or change in the future, particularly in a post-pandemic world.

What role does the real estate market play in the national economy? Clearly, it represents a large chunk of the GDP. Housing, whether individual or multi-family, plays the largest role, although commercial real estate is certainly not insignificant. Because GDP is an overall measure of the value of the nation's production of goods and services, it takes into account all of the activity generated by the real estate industry. This includes the construction sector as well as real estate related consumption of goods and services.

The percentage of GDP represented by real estate construction, both commercial and residential, varies in response to economic conditions. In 2006, it peaked at 8.9% in the United States, obviously reflecting the boom in the housing market. As the housing crisis unfolded, the fallout became particularly evident when the construction industry logged in at a painfully low 4.9% of GDP in 2010. And while the measures show the fluctuations in construction related activity, the impact is felt beyond the construction industry. Real estate construction has a trickle-down effect that is felt throughout the economy. Housing, especially, is linked to the unemployment rate and consumer spending and it certainly is impacted by lending conditions. So, while we might think of real estate as a market unto itself, it plays a significant role in GDP and it is a particularly sensitive measure of overall economic health.

We know that real estate and GDP are inextricably linked. We know that economic factors such as unemployment and lending rates are important in gauging anticipated movement in real estate values. We look to government bonds as a benchmark rate for measuring real estate investment but attempt to also consider the political and economic factors that may impact the bond market. Perhaps most importantly of all, we strive to gauge overall confidence in the economy. Increasing our knowledge of the way the economy works can help us to see the big picture, perhaps providing better insight into market trends. By learning from the past, we can direct our eye to the future of real estate investment with an improved understanding of the markets and, hopefully, a solid foundation upon which to build.

Successful real estate investors well understand the triple benefits of inflation, appreciation, and leverage. When the central bank wants to induce moderate inflation into the general economy, it reduces its target interest rate to encourage borrowing to drive economic growth. People borrow to invest, and also begin shifting assets, in a search for greater yield. This lifts real estate values, the obvious friend to a real estate investor. Additionally, a profitable investment property that is based on sound fundamentals such as location and condition may experience real appreciation in value. When combined with leverage, where a significant amount of the purchase price of the property is financed with a beneficial interest rate and term, the growing value of the asset relative to the capital investment may compound that capital rather quickly. When you add the opportunities for tax deferral, the ability to compound capital is further enhanced.

Many great real estate fortunes have been built on these principles. Yet, when the economy becomes overheated, either generally or in response to an asset bubble, the central bank will tighten, and drive up the interest rate. By then, credit becomes very expensive, if available at all, and that triple benefit becomes a triple negative. That ends a credit bubble, and this cycle has repeated occasionally in our modern times. The Great Recession of 2008–2009 was an example of this, though it was more complex and severe, and the collapse in collateral values destroyed bank assets and, thus, capital. When real estate values climb faster than real GDP, at some point, but inevitably, those values must correct, downwardly and painfully.

Key terms

- **Real Estate**—property consisting of land and buildings.
- **Capitalization of Income**—a type of real estate appraisal method that estimates the value of a property based on the current operating income the property generates.
- **Discounted Cash Flows**—an appraisal method that determines the value of real estate today based on projections of how much income it will generate in the future.
- **Net Operating Income**—total income generated from owning a property minus its associated operating expenses.
- **Capitalization Rate**—the ratio of net operating income to the value of a property.
- **Depreciation**—the reduction in value of real estate over time due to wear and tear.

- **Real Estate Investment Trust**—a company that owns, operates, or finances income-generating real estate.
- **Replacement Rate**—the number of children that a couple would have to have in order to replace themselves.

End-of-chapter problems

1. In any earlier chapter, we examined what bond prices are. Using the same logic as we did for bond prices, what do you think is the relationship between interest rates and house prices? Does this make sense when you think about the impact of the higher interest rate on the mortgage market?

2. If you were considering purchasing a property in order to generate rental income from it, what five factors would you deduct from expected rental income to get to your estimate of net operating income?

3. Suppose you are a property owner renting out your property in a city that enacts rent control measures.

    a. Does rent control raise or lower your estimates of your net operating income?

    b. Assuming rent control will remain in place, what are you likely to do with regard to the upkeep of your property?

4. You are considering purchasing a property for $750,000.

    a. If your rental income is projected at $150,000 per year, and you anticipate annual costs of $75,000 per year, what is your net operating income amount?

    b. Calculate the cap rate on these numbers.

    c. If the interest rate on savings account is 8%, would you purchase the property and rent it out, or would you leave your funds in your savings account?

5. The predominant industry in your area is manufacturing cars:

    a. How might competition with foreign car manufacturers affect property values in your city?

    b. If the car firms in your city are the first to invent and implement a successful driver-less car technology, do you anticipate cap rates rising or falling in the city?

6. Does the invention of short-term rentals through companies such as Airbnb raise or lower the cap rate for an investor, other things equal?

7. If you could go back in history and implement one type of policy—either from the government or from the central bank—in order to stop the housing bubble and its bursting in 2008, what would you recommend, and why?

8. Go the St. Louis Fed's 'FRED' website and find a series for the Case-Shiller quarterly national home price index and compute the correlation

between this series and the median sales prices of houses sold in the U.S. for 2000–2020. What explains the fact that the correlation is not one?

9. If you repeat the exercise in the previous question using the Case-Shiller quarterly 20-city composite home price index, would you expect the correlation to improve or worsen? Verify by actually obtaining the data and calculating this correlation.

10. Suppose the cap rate is 10% and the cost of financing is 7%.

   a. Calculate the spread.
   b. Do you still purchase property if inflation was 2%?
   c. What if inflation was 4%?

10 Oil

Objectives

1. This chapter outlines the five main components to fuel prices, and what factors can change these prices.
2. The supply and demand for fuel and the role of elasticity is examined.
3. We describe how speculators may use oil futures contracts.

Each and every one of us is affected by oil prices. Whether purchasing gas at the pump, heating our homes, or buying vegetables at the grocery store, fuel prices affect us every day. Energy is literally what makes the world work. It is pervasive in our lives, impacting almost everything we do. The price of anything that is manufactured, transported, or eaten is affected by changes in oil prices. And yet, the price of energy, oil in particular, is perhaps one of the most misunderstood concepts in economics. Because of the magnitude of its value to our economy and because it's such a part of our everyday lives, it is especially valuable to us to understand how the price of oil works.

The pricing of oil, and particularly gas at the pump, seems complex, creating confusion for many consumers. What other prices are so publicly and visibly displayed on street corners for all to see as is the case with gasoline? What causes high fuel prices? Do oil speculators manipulate prices or are they determined simply by the laws of supply and demand? And finally, what does the future hold? A shift in oil production and consumption around the world can have a profound effect on the entire global economy. For example, industrial and economic growth in China in recent years naturally resulted in an increase in the country's oil consumption, with that new demand for oil needed to heat factories and fuel manufacturing equipment, which has translated into higher prices around the globe. And while that is simple enough to understand, many wonder why oil prices continually rise faster than other prices over time, even when demand seems to stabilize.

Gas prices deconstructed

We're all familiar with the pain at the pump. Fueled by the price of crude oil, gas prices are an everyday concern for Americans. We are predominantly a society

DOI: 10.4324/9781003251453-13

of automobile lovers and, whether working, playing, or both, we enjoy our cars. Unless you live in an urban area and you are able to rely on walking and public transportation for your daily commute, you are well acquainted with the budgetary impact of powering your vehicle. For those who travel by air, the cost of a flight is directly dependent on oil prices. And the prices we pay for the goods we buy every day are determined with transportation and delivery costs factored in. No one is immune to gas prices. And yet, most people cannot really explain the breakdown of the cost of a gallon of gasoline (or diesel fuel).

There are five main components of the cost of fuel:

1. Cost of crude oil
2. Cost of refinement plus related profits
3. Cost of distribution and marketing plus related profits
4. Cost of storage
5. Taxes

While there are occasional manufacturing or refinement hiccups, generally speaking, production and storage costs are fairly steady. The factor that is routinely responsible for the swings in fuel price is, of course, the cost of crude oil. Marketing and taxes are typically consistent. However, as we all know from watching the news, the price of crude can spike suddenly and annual swings of 25% or more are not atypical. So, if there is a volatile element to fuel prices, the price of crude oil is it. For evidence of this, see the average monthly price of the West Texas Intermediate (WTI) price of crude oil since 2000, seen in Figure 10.1.

The huge decline in the price of crude oil during the Great Recession is particularly noteworthy, but aside from this, we see how volatile the price of oil is each month. But what causes these spikes in oil prices? Are the price swings the result of supply and demand or do they emanate from the activities of the oil speculators that we hear so much about? Let's take a look more closely at this market.

Fundamentals—supply and demand

One of the most basic economic fundamentals is the law of supply and demand. Given a constant supply of a good or service, an increase or decrease in demand for that good or service will push prices up or down, accordingly. If demand is constant, then changes in supply will result in either increasing or decreasing prices. While that rule of thumb is applicable in some capacity to almost any market, there are those who believe that pricing in energy markets is controlled by more than fundamental economic factors. Regardless of any other influences, the truth is the law of supply and demand is at work in the oil market. In fact, the typical annual swings in price can be related directly to seasonal supply and demand shifts.

For example, we know that gas prices in America tend to rise each year around Memorial Day. It is not coincidental that this is the beginning of

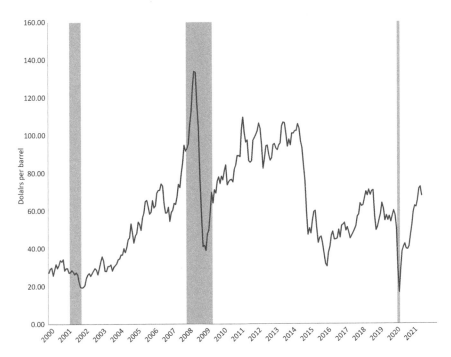

Figure 10.1 West Texas Intermediate Crude Oil Price.
Source: U.S. Energy Information Administration

the summer travel and vacation season. Prices at the pump are higher in summer months because demand for fuel peaks during warmer weather. In addition to increased fuel demand due to vacation travel, some industries, such as construction and tourism, are busier during the warmer seasons of the year. And although winter weather brings with it a higher demand for heating oil, the combined effect of business and personal travel in summer results in a big increase in baseline demand. So, with a relatively constant supply, the fluctuations in price primarily result from seasonal changes in demand. To see this more explicitly, consider Figure 10.2 which shows how the price of fuel rises from P_1 to P_2 after a rise in demand.

While there is a bit of variation, one particular aspect of the market for fuel that is different from some others is constant, fixed demand. Because fuel is a factor across the board and it plays some role in bringing almost every product to market, there is a certain amount of consumption that will remain regardless of price fluctuations. Because of this fixed, baseline amount of demand, there is very limited *price elasticity* in the oil market. Where demand in some industries is highly sensitive to price, fuel sales will not shift as much as a result of a price change.

Consider what would happen if the cost of a movie ticket began to increase: the number of movie goers would decrease as the price ramped upward. At a certain point, maybe $30 or $40 per ticket, theaters might sit

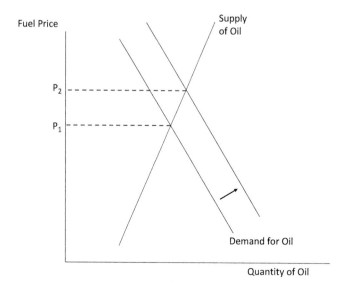

Figure 10.2 Increase in Demand for Fuel.

empty on Friday evenings. Other than movie reviewers, no one needs to go to a movie at that price. The very few patrons who could afford to go and would pay the higher price to see a movie would be insufficient to sustain the cost of keeping theaters in operation.

Going to the movies is a choice, and consumers can opt out of the market. In economics, we say that the demand for movie tickets is *elastic*, meaning demand is very responsive to price changes. Compare that to the market for fuel, where only a portion of demand stems from choice. If you must drive to work, you will purchase fuel. If you must heat your home, especially if you are somewhere in the Northeast U.S. in winter, you will use heating oil. You may opt to skip weekend trips to the mall or set your thermostat to maintain a cooler temperature, but you cannot avoid purchasing at least some fuel, regardless of price. Therefore, the demand for oil is relatively *inelastic*, meaning it is less responsive to changes in price. We can distinguish between elastic and inelastic demand by seeing the slopes of these demand curves, seen in Figure 10.3.

Elastic demand has a flatter slope, whereas inelastic demand is steeper.

The gasoline market has arguably one of the least elastic demand curves relative to price and the industry is well versed in typical consumption patterns. So, if the industry constantly monitors consumption and if seasonal demand is somewhat predictable, why are there unexpected spikes and why did the price of oil increase drastically during the mid-2000s? Well, the other side of the equation is supply. Generally speaking, under normal conditions, the oil industry has a relatively inelastic supply curve. The industry operates

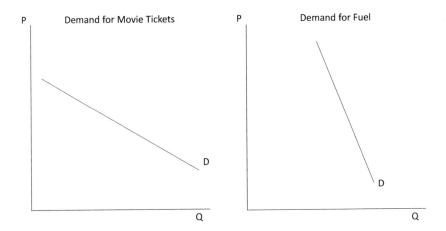

Figure 10.3 Elasticity of Demand.

in such a way as to meet the demand of the economy with an eye toward maximization of profit. If all goes as intended, the economy is happy as consumers are satisfied and the industry hits the sweet spot in regard to profit. Oil tends to flow as needed based on industry experience with a reasonable amount of storage factored in as part of the supply chain management.

Suppliers are tuned into the market and know when it is time to tap new wells. When oil begins to flow, pumping generally continues uninterrupted until the point where producers determine that it is economically beneficial to cap the well. There are routine supply shifts, such as in springtime when refineries temporarily shut down for annual maintenance and to shift over to production of summer grade fuel, which burns cleaner and more efficiently and is kinder to the environment, and helps offset some of the spike in consumption during summer months. Because this timing typically correlates with the beginning of peak travel season, the impact of the supply interruption is anticipated, and the cost is absorbed in the typical summer price increase.

However, not all changes in supply are predictable or expected. Natural disasters such as hurricanes, such as the hit the Gulf of Mexico took in 2005, can affect refinery operations and disrupt supply. Political unrest in oil producing regions of the Middle East always creates uncertainty in regard to oil supply so we generally expect prices to rise along with those news reports. Fear of disruption alone can lead the market to anticipate higher prices.

Given the difference between inelastic and elastic demand, compare how a reduction in supply for movie tickets and gasoline affects prices (see Figure 10.4).

From these diagrams, we can see a far larger change in the price of gasoline (rises to P_3) due to its inelasticity of demand, whereas movie ticket prices change by a much smaller amount (they rise to P_2).

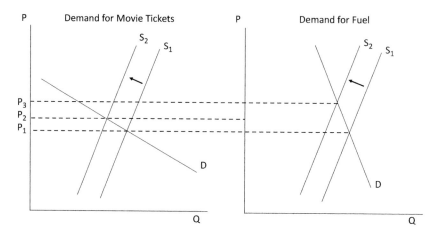

Figure 10.4 Elasticity of Demand and a Change in Supply.

Further, the value of the dollar relative to other world currencies can play into the price of oil. Oil is priced internationally in dollars. When the dollar is strong against a basket of currencies, demand for oil in non-U.S. countries drops, as oil becomes more expensive to them. As demand drops, the price falls. Conversely, if the value of the dollar drops, demand returns in those other countries. Still, all those price spikes are typically explainable and somewhat short-lived, and questions remain when we see fuel prices change, sometimes significantly, seemingly at random. If it is all supply and demand at work, why do we hear about price gouging at the pump? And why is there so much talk about oil speculators?

Is it speculation?

What is oil speculation? If you believe many of the news reports out there, you might believe that there is a concerted effort to influence the oil market by a small group of investors who trade in the oil markets in order to make a quick profit with no regard to the fact that, in the process, they are helping raise fuel prices at the expense of the average consumer. Is that what happens?

Simply stated, speculation is the purchase of an oil-related asset by a party who is anticipating a rise in the price of the asset, producing a capital gain on their investment. Some of those who speculate on oil prices are indeed investors and they are in it only seeking a profit, with no intention of ever taking delivery of a single drop of oil. Others who enter the market have a vested interest in fuel prices for business purposes and are simply looking to hedge, such as an airline attempting to control fuel costs. Some speculators may indeed be willing to purchase oil. While the motivations and intentions of those participating in the speculation market may be different, the mechanics are somewhat similar.

Oil speculation, as a profitable activity, has been actually around for a long time. As a practice, however, it gained popularity among investors outside the oil industry as derivatives products became easily traded on the open market.

Facts about futures

A futures contract falls under the umbrella of derivatives products, meaning that it derives its value from the underlying product itself. And while there are other types of derivatives, we are going to focus on futures contracts for our discussion of oil speculation, as they are arguably the most popular of oil-related investments. In the case of oil futures, the value of the contract changes relative to the value crude oil. The terms of the agreement dictate the purchase and sale of a particular lot of crude oil, typically 1,000 barrels, on a stated future date, at a stated price, with delivery made to a particular refinery.

Traders are motivated to enter into the contracts, whether or not they actually plan to purchase or sell the oil, in order to capitalize on the volatility in the futures market. Basically, if a buyer believes the price of oil is going up, they may want to lock in at a price that is higher than current, or spot, prices but lower than where they think oil will be trading on the maturity date. For example, if you can buy a futures contract for oil at $35 a barrel for a year's time, and you predict that the spot price of oil will be $45 a barrel at that time, you would want to purchase these futures. For a seller, perhaps an oil producer, the reverse is true, with the intention being to lock in at a price above where they expect crude to trade in the future.

Futures contracts are traded on exchanges and settled through a clearing house, making it fairly easy for market participants to execute trades efficiently. Just as with most other commodities futures, contracts turn over many times prior to their actual maturity date, with each seller along the way hoping to make a marginal profit. Rarely does the initial purchaser hold the contract until expiry. The final holder has the option of taking delivery of the oil at the contract price, typically via delivery to a contractually specified refinery, or they can offset their position and accept a cash settlement for the difference between the stated contract price and the spot price on that date. As a matter of practice, it is quite rare, coming in around less than 2%, for futures traders to actually take possession of oil upon the maturity of a contract. The remaining 98% typically settles for cash, leaving the actual supply of oil untouched.

If the supply and demand equilibrium is largely unaffected, why do we see so many newspaper articles making the case that speculation drives oil prices up? A look at the mechanics makes it clear that the source of profits for traders is the purchase and sale of the contracts themselves. The futures market, unlike other commodity or equity markets, revolves purely around the trading of the paper contracts, with nothing being purchased upon entry into the market.

If you purchase stock, you are actually buying an asset that represents a share of a company. In the futures market, you simply make a deposit in a margin account, somewhat like an entry fee, which allows you to play. Then, you enter into an agreement for a future purchase or sale of a commodity. You haven't actually purchased anything yet. Your margin account is adjusted as the value of the paper changes daily. You can trade your contract for another, taking a marginal profit or loss, or you can hold it until maturity, at which time you will most likely settle out by way of adjustment to your margin account. At no time during that process did you take ownership of any oil.

So, how could you be blamed for causing an increase in the price of crude? In a sense, the futures market operates apart from and independently of the oil market. The two are linked because the futures trading prices are based on the price of crude and the value of the contracts will fluctuate along with crude, but the trading of futures contracts operates within its own system and responds to its own intrinsic forces of supply and demand. Unless the oil industry players are actually participating in futures market itself, which they sometimes do to hedge against falling prices, they do not stand to incur any profit or loss from the trades. And unless speculators take delivery of the oil, actually storing it and thereby removing it from the supply chain, they cannot affect the supply side of the market. As for the demand side of the equilibrium, the fact that less than 2% of speculative contracts result in the holder taking delivery makes it pretty clear that the majority of speculators have no direct impact on the amount of crude being by the market.

To store or not to store

So, what about storage? If we contend that speculators can only affect oil prices by taking delivery of oil, can a small group of speculators create enough of a supply chain disruption to impact the price we pay at the pump? Should we fear oil hoarding by the market? While taking delivery actually entails ownership of oil that is physically being delivered to a stated refinery, at the end of the day, the speculator can dictate when that refined product hits the market. In the meantime, they must provide for physical storage of the product, either renting space from an oil company or dictating delivery to their own vessel. That is pretty impractical for a non-industry speculator.

Whether in above-ground tanks or a fleet of ocean-borne tankers, oil storage is costly. It is a necessary part of the infrastructure for those in the industry and we can be certain that they know exactly which levels to target for profit maximization. Thus, it would not be in their best interests to hoard oil in any significant fashion. And, while the most cost-effective storage is in the ground, once a well begins flowing, it is economically disadvantageous to temporarily cap it in order to alter supply. So, it is unlikely that an oil company will hoard oil, whether in tanks or by disrupting extraction processes.

Further, although oil industry participants do speculate from time to time, most players are hedge funds and brokerage firms. They clearly would not be experts at oil storage and the added cost would erode potential profits, making them less likely to accept the exposure for not only security but also environmental risks. While it can be marginally profitable on occasion for a speculator to arrange, in some way, for storage of oil, the associated costs and risks make it unlikely that it will remain a profitable long-term activity. So, we can surmise that, for some, it may be an opportunistic endeavor and they may get lucky on occasion, but the inherent risks of storing oil make it almost always a short-lived activity. As a long-term business model, oil storage is only practical for those in the industry.

Speculation and oil prices

By addressing the impracticality of the storage issue, can we effectively dismiss the accusations of those who contend that oil speculators are directly responsible for price gouging at the pump? Not exactly. Speculation likely has influenced the crude oil market, even pricing, in a small way. How? Well, as we outlined, a few speculators do take delivery of oil and they probably have some impact on supply and demand. While difficult to quantify, it is probably safe to say that the effect made by less than 2% of the volume of futures is largely insignificant.

Even if speculators decided suddenly to store an unusually and unexpectedly large volume of oil on a fleet of tankers, the impact of their decision would be temporary. Initially, prices would rise in response to the decrease in supply, but the market would shift over time as the industry gradually picked up production and covered the shortage. Then, assuming prices returned to equilibrium, the reintroduction of the stored oil into the market would ostensibly cause prices to decrease, returning to natural market levels.

Of course, that is market theory and it would likely not happen that smoothly. The speculators responsible for storing the oil would target the sale of their hoarded oil and attempt to enter it into the supply chain at a time when prices were peaking. And the industry would likely react to the availability of that oil by adjusting supply, preventing prices from bottoming out so suddenly that consumers begin lining up at the pumps. Eventually, though, equilibrium would return, and prices would settle out close to where they would otherwise have been all along, as ultimately determined by the interplay of supply and demand. The same scenario would be true if the oil producers themselves decided to restrict supply, only to release it to the market later. Eventually, natural market forces push prices back toward equilibrium.

All of this is corroborated by the fact that oil inventories have remained relatively consistent. If there were huge profits to be had by hoarding oil, increases in inventories would be evident during times when oil prices peaked. Since there is no evidence of this happening, it is unlikely that there is a significant amount of storage manipulation in the market. So, while there may be some short-term impact on oil prices caused by the speculators who choose to take delivery of oil, it is unlikely that long-term prices are affected in any meaningful way.

Market signals

What about the theory that momentum in the futures markets has an effect on the price of crude? The theory is that the issuance of an unusually large volume of contracts sends a signal to the oil industry that the market anticipates price movement of a certain direction. The contention is that oil producers respond to that message, particularly by hoarding oil with the intention of selling it later when prices are expected to be higher. The decreased supply would drive up current prices at the pump. Unlike an outside speculator who stores oil, industry insiders would have the power to control the overall oil supply.

If we stop there, it seems logical that speculators could be indirectly affecting prices at the gas pump. But we must consider that the oil industry can certainly not react overnight to fluctuations in the futures market. And that market fluctuates rapidly. A bubble could form simply based on excessive optimism in the futures market, driven by both experienced and unsophisticated investors alike. What basis is there for oil industry executives to gamble with profits based on bubbles that could pop without warning? That isn't to say that oil producers ignore market patterns. But oil companies are typically going to have the most accurate information about their own industry, and they will probably trust their own data over the reactions of speculative traders.

Back to supply and demand

If speculation was not the driving force behind the run-up in oil prices in the recent past, what was? To answer that question, we return to the rapid industrialization in China, India, and other emerging markets. Figure 10.5 shows energy consumption by countries and regions published by the Energy Information Administration (EIA), where we see rapid growth in China and India's energy usage.

Simply put, the world began to demand more oil. Supply, being largely inelastic, could not meet the overall global demand so prices were pushed up and the available supplies went to the highest bidders. While this may initially take us by surprise, in hindsight, we can see this is a classic example of the fundamentals of supply and demand at work in market. The only way the oil industry could meet the sudden, increased demand for oil coming from developing nations was to redirect some of the supply that would otherwise be available to everyone else.

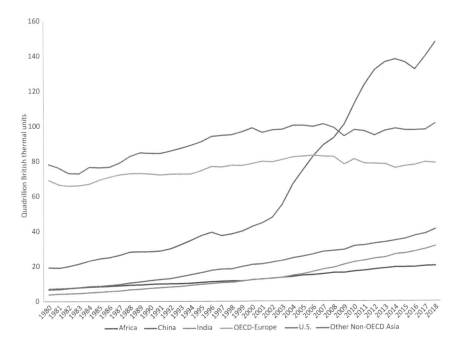

Figure 10.5 Total Energy Consumption in Selected Countries and Regions, 1980–2018.
Source: U.S. Energy Information Administration

Why did prices spike so much in 2008 at a time when the economy was on the brink of recession? As we know, demand is not highly sensitive to price changes, so it takes quite an increase before we reduce our fuel consumption. Prices had to rise enough to cause consumers to take notice and adapt accordingly. Now, we know that the spike in oil prices leveled off and actually came back down. That is partially due to eventual production increases by the oil industry but also is attributable to the economic woes from the global recession, slowing growth and causing fuel demands to taper.

Peak oil

If the law of supply and demand is the primary driver of oil prices, then what would happen if we suddenly found out that the global supply of oil has reached its peak and would soon begin to contract? That very question is something that economists are faced with as the scientific community continues to warn us of the finite nature of our oil supply. *Peak oil* is an industry term typically used to refer to the point at which an oil well, or an entire oil field, reaches its maximum rate of production. After peak oil is reached, the rate of production begins to decline until the point at which it is no longer economically feasible to extract oil from the well, or field, in question.

When we hear the term *Peak Oil* in the mainstream media, it is usually alongside dire warnings of the economic catastrophe believed to be looming in our oil-dependent future. As the theory goes, our global consumption of oil is moving at such a rapid pace that we are on target to run out of the resource in the near future. Is there a scientific basis for concern or is the peak oil theory an attempt by the oil industry to support higher prices?

The theory of peak oil is not new. Coined by geoscientist M. King Hubbert in the 1950s, the concept suggests that oil production on a global scale follows a bell-shaped curve, similar to the pattern of production from a single oil well or field. Known as the Hubbert Curve, it illustrates that global oil production has increased on a gradual scale and will eventually reach a point of maximum production. After reaching this peak, the rate of production will begin to fall until it ultimately reaches a terminal point. So, when referencing the studies of Mr. Hubbert, the term *peak oil* refers to the point at which the world reaches its maximum oil productivity. From a scientific and economic standpoint, it not only refers to attaining peak productivity but also applies to the ensuing economic effects of the *post-peak* period.

And, make no mistake, there would be economic effects. The suggestion that oil production has reached its maximum rate would set the stage for increasing energy prices, rationing of fuel, the expectation of hoarding, and probable security and defense challenges that would emerge along with fear of a future without fossil fuels. Economic confidence would nosedive, and the possibility of a global recession would set in. It is a perfect example of the law of supply and demand at work in the market.

This is no hypothetical scenario. The question is not if peak oil will be reached, but *when*. Science confirms that oil is a non-renewable resource, as its formation requires specific geological circumstances and periods of time. Since, in economic terms, peak oil is not about the certainty of whether we will eventually exhaust our stores of oil as much as the severity of the economic reaction to having hit the pinnacle of production and the fallout that will follow as supplies diminish, the debate revolves around attempts at answering critical questions like the following:

- What if we develop alternatives to oil as an energy resource, thereby reducing our dependence on fossil fuels?
- What if we improve our energy efficiency significantly, thereby decreasing our overall rate of consumption of oil?
- What if the point of peak oil is not a short-lived pinnacle but more of a plateau that lasts for a while?

Any of these factors, as well as many others, could alter the economic impact of reaching peak oil production. We might still see rising prices for crude but that may have less effect on the broad economy if we are relying less on oil and more on renewable energy sources such as wind or solar. Clearly, there is no debate as to the fact that oil stores can eventually be depleted. But the impact that this has on us in terms of our economic stability is yet to be determined.

At the heart of the matter is the question of when we will reach the top of the bell curve. There are multiple theories addressing the time frame for reaching peak oil, with some predicting that we will be there in the next 10 years. Yet, there are more questions than answers and it is difficult to rely on any one study. And perhaps it is best if we do not know how long we have. If we fear that we are speeding toward imminent crisis, we will be more driven to find alternatives rather than pace ourselves, knowing that there is time to spare. Adaptation generally occurs in response to necessity. We are not waiting for science to tell us that the time for action is coming. We are frantically searching for new ways to tap otherwise unreachable oil resources.

Innovation, many believe, will produce alternatives that eliminate our reliance on oil as our primary fuel source altogether, thereby ending the economic crisis before it starts. If these things come to pass, perhaps we may never deplete the world's stores of oil. Thus, the reason some people are debunking the applicability of peak oil theory altogether. Scientists are working every day to improve existing energy practices and develop new ones, leading most experts believe that peak oil production will not come as soon as previously forecasted and that, when it does come, it will have far less economic impact than previous predictions implied. The key point is to understand how the theory of peak oil applies in terms of economic impact. Then, we can apply our understanding of the way the oil market works, based on the fundamentals of supply and demand, to guide us in making our own financial decisions.

Future demand and alternative energy sources

Projecting into the future, no one can say with certainty what fuel prices are expected to do. We know that world oil stores remain abundant for now and we are constantly coming up with new ways to tap into oil reserves. Typically, oil extraction reaches its maximum production when about 50% of the oil is pumped from a particular well. And wells are never completely exhausted. At some point, extraction reaches a point at which it is no longer economically advantageous to continue pumping and a well is then capped. Thus, there are substantial stores of oil that are effectively inaccessible. For many years, it has been more efficient to simply move on to the next source rather than find new ways to extract remaining oil from previously tapped wells.

Now, however, economic and political conditions are making it a priority to develop methods of reaching these remaining stores of fossil fuel. Fracking, which involves extracting oil from shale and is probably the most well-known of these methods, is controversial but seems promising in terms of oil production. Much research is being focused on the environmental impacts of fracking, in hopes that it will be a developed into a viable alternative for the future of the industry.

If the price of oil had never increased, perhaps we would still not be focused on alternative means of oil extraction. But we consumers are motivated by our wallets and it is no surprise that we are now dedicating renewed efforts to finding alternative sources of energy. And, whether it is fracking or another method of accessing oil reserves, we can assume that we will find a way to free up previously unreachable stores of fossil fuel. Still, there will come a time when the availability of oil becomes a concern. That is the catalyst for the race that is occurring within the scientific community to find alternative ways to power our world.

As with so many past dilemmas, we will surely innovate our way to a solution to our energy problems. Future generations will likely be far less dependent on oil. For now, however, we remain beholden to fossil fuels, making the price of crude an ongoing area of focus and fear. By understanding the true forces at work in the oil market, we can hopefully filter out the hype and make thoughtful and wise decisions in our own economic lives.

Key terms

- **Price Elasticity of Demand**—the variation in demand for a good or service as a result of a change in the price of that same good or service.
- **Price Elasticity of Supply**—a measure of the responsiveness of the quantity of a good or service supplied as a result of a change in the price of that same good or service.
- **Derivative**—a financial security whose return is derived from another asset.
- **Futures Contract**—a type of derivative where a buyer and seller agree to a trade at a predetermined future date at a predetermined price.
- **Peak Oil**—the point at which an oil well or field reaches its maximum rate of production.

End-of-chapter problems

1. Go to the St. Louis Fed's "FRED" website and download data on the WTI price of crude oil from 2000 to 2020.

   a. When did the largest one-year drop in the price of oil occur and by how much?
   b. Can you think of some reasons that caused this decline?

2. Do the following goods and services likely have elastic or inelastic demand?

   a. Drinking water.
   b. Football jerseys.
   c. Electricity.
   d. Children's toys.

3. Consider the market for airplane tickets where there are two types of traveler: a businessperson and a vacationer.

   a. Which of the two types of traveler likely has a more elastic demand for plane tickets?
   b. Draw the demand curves for these two travelers.
   c. Suppose a new regulation is passed by Congress that forces airlines to retire any airplanes that were produced over 10 years ago. Using a supply curve together with the demand curves you drew in (b), show whether the impact on ticket prices is greater for the businessperson or the vacationer.

4. Imagine we live in a world where cars are the only form of transportation and are necessary to get from point A to point B.

   a. Will the demand for gasoline be elastic or inelastic?
   b. Over time, electric cars are invented. Will the demand curve for gasoline get flatter or steeper?
   c. Can we expect more or less volatile gasoline prices when electric cars are invented?

5. You currently possess 100 barrels of oil and the spot price of oil is $40 a barrel. You do your homework and predict that the oil barrel price will be $50 in 30 days' time. A domestic gasoline company is interested in buying your oil in 30 days' time. Assuming no transaction costs would you agree to sell if they offer a price of:

   a. $45 per barrel?
   b. $55 per barrel?
   c. If someone from the future comes to you in a time machine and tells you that the actual price will be $42 in 30 days' time, what do you now think of the $45 and $55 per barrel offers?

6. You run a bakery that requires lots of flour every day. The current market price of flour is $0.50 per pound. A national flour producer offers to sell you a forward contract of 100 pounds of flour next year at a price of $0.55 per pound of flour. Do you accept this deal if you suspect the price of flour next year will be:

   a. $0.52 per pound?
   b. $0.56 per pound?

7. Assume there is a fixed global supply of oil in 2020:

   a. Draw this supply curve on a diagram.
   b. Where would the demand curves for the United States, China, and India lie, given what Figure 10.5 suggests? Draw your answer.

8. Suppose an oil well has been extracted, although there is still some un-tapped oil remaining in reserve:

    a.   What must be true of the expected revenue from that oil that is in the ground versus the expected costs of drilling for that oil?

    b.   If you ran an oil extraction company, would you seek to develop technology to extract the remainder of the oil? What must be true of the expected revenue and the expected costs of the technological investment to drive your decision? How does the current market price of oil influence your decision?

11 Gold

Objectives

1. We study the uniqueness of gold as an asset relative to other assets.
2. The advantages and disadvantages of viewing gold as an investment are discussed.
3. We consider the gold standard in further detail. The reasons as to why a return to the gold standard is unlikely are detailed.
4. We study how speculation can undermine and destabilize a fixed exchange rate regime.

If you have ever watched American television at all, you've may have seen one of the commercials featuring television personalities or celebrities who issue dire warnings that an economic collapse of epic proportions is imminent and advise viewers to protect themselves by buying gold. There are similar advertisements that surface on the internet, often with video presentations making the case for gold as the only sure way to avoid economic disaster. Do these people really know something that the rest of us do not? Common sense tells us that the only reason these ads exist is because someone, aside from the actors being paid to get our attention, is making money from them. But the videos are compelling, and fear is a powerful motivator. While a reasonably intelligent person can see through this hype, it is understandable that there is still much confusion about gold. To make sense of it, we must filter out the emotion and present the facts in a framework that simplifies how we should think about gold.

Gold does not have much relevance in our daily lives. We could easily live without it. But gold has a mystique about it that makes it unique. We revere gold for its lasting sense of value and the weight it carries in our minds. No other tangible thing, metal or otherwise, has captured our imaginations through the ages as has gold. In large part, this stems from the fact that gold once was a predominant form of money (a type of *commodity money*). It still is respected as a store of value because it is somewhat accepted as a medium of exchange. From a purely technical standpoint, it could still function as money, but it is not an efficient or practical form of money. It is quite bulky

DOI: 10.4324/9781003251453-14

to carry around and you can't exactly use it at the gas pump or the grocery store. Thus, it is not very relevant to us as we go about our daily routines.

If gold is impractical as money, why do we place it on such a high pedestal? Consider what images come to mind when you think about gold. Most people envision gold bars, gold coins, or jewelry. Some of us might have a ring or watch or some other piece made of gold, perhaps a beautiful heirloom passed down to us from previous generations. If you let your mind go back in time, visions of pirates with treasure chests of gold coins come to mind. History books show pictures of Egyptian Pharaohs with layers of ornate gold embellishments. So, as a culture, we are programmed to think of gold as valuable and lasting. And it does have lasting value. Gold never becomes obsolete. We would never just throw away a piece of gold like we do so many other things. That alone tells us that gold behaves a bit differently than most other asset classes. And we must think differently about it, separate the feelings from the facts, and take an objective look at the true value of gold.

Value and confidence

Let's start with some basic facts. Gold is almost impossible to oxidize or corrode. An atom of gold is always going to be an atom of gold. Separating the electrons from the nucleus of an atom of gold is more difficult to accomplish than for most other elements in the universe.

Gold can be melted and alloyed with other metals. That alloy can then be melted again and returned to its pure gold atomic form. This means if gold were ever mined in the world's history, it is still with us either in an industrial or electrical device, in a gold coin, a bar of gold in your safe deposit box, in the central banks' vaults, in the filling in your tooth, a necklace around your neck, or the wedding band on your finger.

How much gold is there? According to the World Gold Council, if all the gold in the world was gathered, melted, and formed into a single cube, that cube would measure about 69 feet per side. And, interestingly, that represents a little less than 1 ounce per person in the world. What is it worth? You could calculate it daily if you cared to, but on any given day, it would be worth about 10 trillion dollars, give or take a trillion or so. That's a lot of money in one sense, given that it may be about half of the annual GDP of the United States, or about one-tenth of the world's GDP.

Consider Figure 11.1 that displays the monthly gold price from 2000 to 2020. Notice how gold frequently rises sharply in price during periods of recession. We see this in the Great Recession of 2008–2009, particularly in the second half of that recession, and we see it noticeably during the 2020 Covid-19-induced recession. We can also observe that the gold price during the height of the 2020 recession is over double what it was during the height of the Great Recession.

Why these spikes in price? At some level, fear seems to play a role. Clearly, the 2008–2013 period was wrought with economic stress and worry. After the global financial crisis, many were concerned about financial stability and

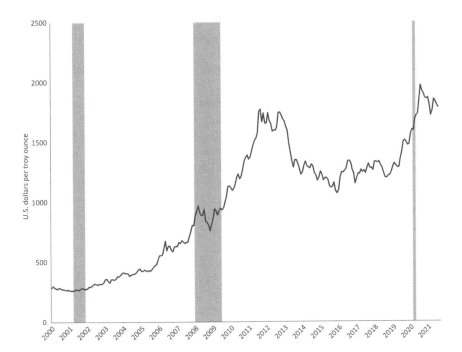

Figure 11.1 Gold Price.
Source: ICE Benchmark Administration

security, with workers facing unemployment and displacement as jobs disappeared and homes went into foreclosure. In the United States, Gallup's Economic Confidence Index, which bases its measure on (1) the perception of current economic conditions and (2) whether the economy is getting better or worse, reached its lowest point in 2008. The Consumer Confidence Index, as measured by The Confidence Board, reported similar results, with the CCI reflecting dramatically low readings in the fourth quarter of 2008. Since the price of gold can be viewed as a *barometer of confidence*, it is no surprise that the gold market began a steady upward climb around that same time.

Gold trades primarily on fear rather than any real economic fundamentals. When economic troubles arise and confidence is eroded, gold becomes a safe haven for those who believe that it has stable, intrinsic value. But, does that make it a good investment? How should we look at gold as an asset class? Are there real reasons to include gold in an investment portfolio?

Is gold an investment?

Should we buy gold? Should a percentage of our savings be allocated to gold as a hedge against inflation? Let's consider that gold, as an asset, behaves differently than other classes of assets. There are several reasons for this.

Primarily, consider that gold is not exactly an investment in the sense that it provides no real return or income. Yes, there are hedge funds based on gold positions and you can consider the fact that gold may increase in value, thereby providing a gain if you sell it, but simply holding an amount of gold does not provide the purchaser with any immediate return. Thus, it behaves in a sense like the commodity that it is.

But while it fits the definition of a commodity, it is not typical in the way that other commodities are valued, making it a bit of a maverick. Because gold is also viewed as a form of money, its price is driven somewhat by the belief that it has a stable value. Further, there is confidence that the market for gold will always exist, eliminating the fear that plagues other commodities markets. The fact that gold can be exchanged into money with some expectation of reliability adds a premium to the value that it would otherwise hold. Since gold is not purely speculative in nature, many see it as a way to secure the value of their savings in an environment of economic uncertainty. And, although the basic rules of supply and demand do come into play, the value of gold is also affected by psychological perceptions.

When inflation is anticipated and the value of the dollar is falling, gold prices tend to rise. Initially, this has nothing to do with the supply of gold. It is merely a reaction to the perceived loss of value of the dollar. Of course, when more people begin to come into the gold market, the increasing demand continues to drive the price upward. As previously mentioned, economic confidence was at a low in 2008. Due to the severity of the recession and the fear that policies such as Quantitative Easing would lead to inflation, gold began an upward run that lasted well into 2013, outperforming most other asset classes during that period. Clearly, this was a reaction to fear and uncertainty, not any real fundamentals of the gold market itself. So, while those who bought gold may have profited, they did so only because individuals were paralyzed with fear and, for many, confidence in the future was eroded.

So, what about those television commercials? They make it sound as if gold is the only way to ensure financial security. Certainly, many of those who flocked to gold in its recent heyday did feel quite pessimistic about the future of the global economy. All of us were concerned about where the world was headed. But, in terms of how we invest money and where we allocate our savings, we must remember to maintain balance. Investment advisors typically recommend some diversification in a portfolio with periodic rebalancing. Many advise that some income producing stocks and a small percentage of cash be held along with a small position in gold or some other commodity as a hedge. But, the majority of a typical investment portfolio is generally allocated to growth stocks.

What does this tell us? It's all about confidence! If you view growth stocks as a belief in the productive future of the economy, it translates as a belief that the economy will grow. Hence, it is basically a statement of confidence in the future. So, those who advocate hoarding gold are banking on fear.

They are buying into a pessimistic view of not only the economy but also the overall spirit of the human race. They are gambling on the likelihood of the long-term economic failure. Yes, there are economic downturns and, yes, there are political hurdles along the way. But buying into the idea that the sky is falling is like making a bet that we will fail to overcome those downturns and hurdles.

All of this makes it sound as if it is wrong to buy gold. However, it really is not a political statement at all. Gold is not a bad thing to own, it is simply unproductive. It has some value as a commodity and its use in certain sectors of manufacturing certainly can be productive. But buying a bar of gold is not a true investment and dumping large amounts of savings into gold as an inflation hedge is based on fear. It is a bet against the ability of the innovative and productive endeavors of our modern economy to continue to innovate and grow. Don't let the fear of economic collapse drive us to buy into the hype when history tells us that productivity and ingenuity are better long-term bets than bars of gold will ever be. And really, how practical is it to carry around gold?

In truth, if a catastrophic event did occur, causing the economy to completely collapse and devaluing the dollar completely, the least practical thing anyone would trade for would be gold. What would they do with it? Who would accept it, anyway? Most likely, we would be bartering food for weapons or some other means of providing security amid the chaos, not gold coins or bars.

The gold standard

Typically, something that we hear referenced in sound bites around election time, the Gold Standard is defined by the Library of Economics and Liberty as a *commitment by participating countries to fix the prices of their domestic currencies in terms of a specified amount of gold.* If a country adheres to a gold standard, that country's currency, both national notes and bank deposits, could theoretically be redeemed at a specified price for gold. Throughout history, many countries, including the United States, have operated under a gold standard system at some time, although no country currently does so. Lacking a monetary system based on gold, or any other resource, most currencies are a type of *fiat currency*, or money declared to be legal tender by the government but lacking intrinsic value.

Would a return to a gold standard stabilize the value of our currency, or any country's currency, and is it possible? This is a question often posed in political and economic discussions. In fact, some very noteworthy people are staunch supporters of the idea that countries should return to a modified currency standard based on the price of gold. What does this mean, exactly? Well, the basic premise is that the value of the dollar would be fixed to the value of a specific weight in gold. Essentially, the value of all goods and services would be measured based on the value of gold, with legal currency such as the U.S. dollar simply being used to represent that value. Technically, since the United States and other countries would be fixing the price of gold, this implies a system of fixed exchange rates between these countries, something that is not well understood by most people today who advocate for a return to the gold standard. As with most things, there are strong opinions on both sides of the gold standard argument, and it can often be confusing.

Supporters argue that gold is an appropriate anchor of value because it is a non-renewable resource with a fixed, known quantity and they believe that a policy equating dollars with a fixed weight of gold would thus help stabilize the value of the dollar and other world currencies. An essential element of the gold standard is that the supply of dollars would be fixed to the value of gold. Therefore, proponents suggest that if a large economy such as the United States once again adopted a gold standard, the system would impose restraint on the Federal Reserve and their expansion of money supply. For those who mistrust the Fed, this sounds like a good plan.

But would returning to a gold standard solve the problem? The gold standard could limit the Fed's expansion of reserves and perhaps it could potentially discipline government spending too, but we would also face some undesirable trade-offs. Namely, a return to the gold standard would limit many actions of national economic policies that most people find beneficial. These limitations built into the system were much of the reason that the United States, as well as other countries, moved away from the gold standard in the past. And the rigidity of the system does not necessarily impart good behavior any more than the mere existence of laws forces citizens to follow them. In fact, past failures under the gold standard were due in part to deficit spending and corruption. So, clearly, the restrictive nature of the system did not prevent misbehavior in the past. There is nothing to say things would be different in the future.

In addition, the gold standard era should not necessarily be considered as the 'good old days' as it is by many—remember, the gold standard was in use during the Great Depression, which is when we saw sharply negative inflation rates (called 'deflation') which ended up exacerbating the recession further. Research in economics strongly makes the case that this was not coincidental, and the gold standard is likely, at least partially, to blame for these periods of severe economic hardship (for instance, see Mazumder and Wood (2013), "The Great Deflation of 1929–33: It (almost) had to happen," *The Economic History Review*).

In truth, the adoption of a gold standard would likely not change economic behavior that is baked into our belief system and our habits. And it is naïve to think that conversion to a gold standard would suddenly change political behavior. A country's monetary system is simply a product of its nation's citizens and their chosen leaders. If they were motivated to act a certain way, preferably honorably and for the overall good, they would do so under the fiat currency system that we have. If the system is broken or corrupt, it is due to the actions of those in leadership positions and the behavior of those who participate in the system with significant impact. At the end of the day, it all comes down to choices made by individuals. And we sometimes do not follow the rules. So, while the return to a gold standard might impose more restrictions on human behavior, it would not necessarily curtail the actions of those who are determined to go against the rules.

How about economic security? Gold standard proponents argue that economic bubbles can be avoided if there are controls on the rate of growth in the economy. Would that help avoid wild swings in values and prevent recessions? There may be less opportunity for bubbles and perhaps the economy would grow at a more consistent pace. But that potential for predictability comes at a price. Anytime you attempt to control growth, you also restrict flexibility. And we must remember that economic security is affected by more than inflation and inconsistent growth in values.

Where a fiat currency system provides flexibility that enables the issuing country to intervene in times of recession or national crisis, a country operating under a gold standard is held economically captive based on the value of gold. With a fiat currency, policymakers can step in and authorize new currency issues when necessary to mitigate recessionary trends, preventing fallout such as price instability or unemployment. Where a sovereign currency issuer enjoys the benefits of floating exchange rates, a gold standard prevents central bank intervention, making a country operating at a trade deficit particularly vulnerable to recession. This most certainly would affect countries like the United States and is one of the reasons that a return to a gold standard is unlikely.

Perhaps the biggest reason that the gold standard will likely remain a thing of the past is the fact that it limits economic expansion and significantly curbs the ability of our monetary policymakers to react promptly with actions when needs arise. If the country was headed into recession, the central bank would be unable, under a gold standard, to immediately expand the pool of reserves. They would also be unable enact measures to prop up failing banks or preserve certain industries, leading to potentially disastrous economic consequences. And, while it should be noted that some advocates maintain that emergency response powers could be built into a gold-based system, there would still be significant limitations on economic expansion.

The restrictions that are hailed as being the way to prevent economic bubbles would also limit what may be healthy and appropriate economic growth. In the modern technological age in which we live, industries can change, and new product lines may spring up rapidly with innovation. Restricting the ability of certain sectors of the economy to adapt and grow could stunt GDP and the ability of the country to compete on a global, technological scale.

Indeed, in our modern economy, a nation cannot abdicate its responsibility to manage its monetary policy, or control choices made by its citizens, by tying its currency to gold. Good stewardship should be practiced regardless of the system being followed. Thus, as we have argued, the return to a gold standard is probably difficult, and even undesirable, because it takes away the power for us to use monetary policy in an autonomous way to help protect against macroeconomic shocks. In particular, we would be unable to expand the reserve pool to stimulate the economy when there is a recession, since the central bank must primarily use monetary policy to maintain the fixed price of gold above all else.

There are two other reasons why a return to the gold standard is not practical. First, there simply is not enough gold. Perhaps we had enough gold during the classical gold standard in the late nineteenth century, but populations and incomes have grown ever since, while the stock of gold—for obvious reasons—has not grown at the same rate. Second, since a gold standard is a system of fixed exchange rates, it is prone to speculative attacks against the fixed exchange rate, which has caused many fixed exchange rate systems in the past to cease from existence.

Speculative attacks against a fixed exchange rate

To see this last point more clearly, recall the interest parity condition between the United States and United Kingdom:

$$R_{US} = R_{UK} + (X^e - X)/X$$

If we are under a gold standard and the exchange rate is fixed, then $X^e = X$, so the interest parity condition just becomes $R_{US} = R_{UK}$. Then, suppose that a group of traders, for whatever reason, whether warranted or not, starts to believe that the nation will devalue its price of gold, perhaps because they are running low on gold reserves. This causes X^e to rise, which in the foreign exchange diagram would typically cause depreciation of the exchange rate to X_2 (see Figure 11.2).

However, under a gold standard, the central bank cannot let X_1 deviate from its fixed level, so will have to raise the interest rate to $R_{US,2}$ to prevent the exchange rate from changing. What is the problem here? In order to raise the interest rate, the central bank had to lower the money supply and thus lower gold reserves. So, the problem was that gold reserves were low in the first place which prompted expected gold devaluation, but in the process of trying to fix the exchange rate, the central bank must actually lower gold reserves. This causes X^e to rise again, and a vicious cycle has now begun for the central bank to try to defend the fixed exchange rate (Figure 11.3).

In essence, this speculation amounts to a 'run' on the fixed exchange rate. Usually, the best option in this situation is to abandon the fixed exchange rate—and the gold standard—altogether, and to let the currency float.

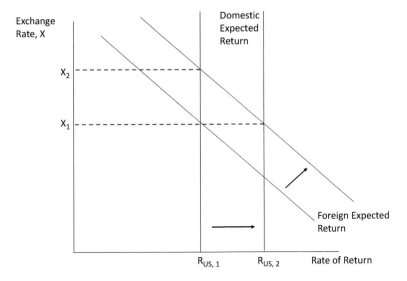

Figure 11.2 Fixing the Exchange Rate after Suspected Devaluation.

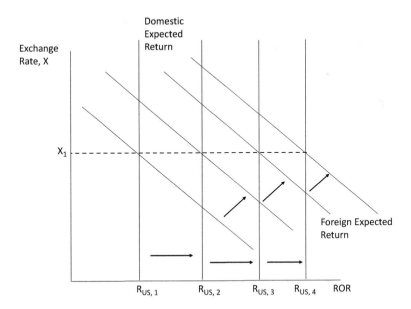

Figure 11.3 Speculative Attack on a Fixed Exchange Rate.

What does the future hold?

None of us can be certain what future events will unfold, but most believe that the fiat currency system is here to stay. In the United States, the decision to abandon the Gold Standard was made deliberately. In the midst of the Great Depression, the U.S. economy was failing miserably, driving many citizens to cash in their dollar denominated deposits for gold. Americans had lost faith in the economy. President Franklin D. Roosevelt's decision to cut the dollar's tie to gold in 1933 enabled Congress to inject money into the system, lowering interest rates and restoring economic confidence. The move is credited by many economists as the single most important act to bring the country out of depression. Yes, some ties to gold remained until the 1970s, but the gold standard had been abandoned and hindsight validates that the decision paved the way for prosperity.

Gold is many things—a beautiful metal, an excellent conductor, a vintage heirloom, a store of value—but it is not a fool proof investment. It is a commodity whose value is determined not by pure fundamentals such as supply and demand, but by reference to its perceived worth as money and by psychological factors such as fear and uncertainty. To help put into perspective that gold is only worth what people think it is worth, and that it has little utility in the real world, consider the words of one of the wealthiest individuals in the world, Warren Buffett:

> *Gold gets dug out of the ground in Africa, or someplace. Then we melt it down, dig another hole, bury it again and pay people to stand around guarding it. It has no utility. Anyone watching from Mars would be scratching their head.*

Key terms

- **Commodity Money**—money that has intrinsic value, such as gold.
- **Fiat Money**—money without intrinsic value, namely paper money.
- **Speculative Attack**—when speculators attack the currency of a country trying to maintain a fixed exchange rate. If the country does not hold enough foreign currency reserves, they may fail to preserve the fixed exchange rate.

End-of-chapter problems

1. Briefly describe how gold does or does not conform to the:

   a. Functions of money.
   b. Ideal characteristics of money.

2. As of 2019, about 195,000 tons of gold have been mined in history. In 1950, that number was roughly 130,000. Over the same time span, world

GDP grew from approximately $1 trillion to about $88 trillion, while the global population grew from about 2.5 billion people to about 8 billion.

   a. Calculate the growth rate in the amount of gold, world GDP, and global population from 1950 to 2019.

   b. Calculate the amount of gold per person over 1950–2019.

   c. What do the numbers from (a) and (b) tell you about the feasibility of operating a gold standard today?

3. Imagine the world operates under a gold standard where they are fixing their price of gold in terms of their own currency. The U.S. price of gold is $20.67 per ounce, and the British price is £4.25 per ounce.

   a. Suppose your local currency market is offering you an exchange rate of $5 to each £1. Can you make a profit from this exchange rate?

   b. What is the exchange rate where the market should settle?

4. A country operates under a gold standard and is fixing their price at 50 per ounce of gold in terms of their own currency. However, they are running very low on gold reserves. What can they do to their price of gold in order to compensate for their low stock of gold reserves?

5. Figure 11.4 shows the gold price against an index of consumer sentiment from 2000 to 2020.

—— Gold Fixing Price 3:00 P.M. (London ▨me) in London Bullion Market, based in U.S. Dollars, U.S. Dollars per Troy Ounce, Daily, Not Seasonally Adjusted
—— University of Michigan: Consumer Sen▨ment, Index 1966:Q1=100, Monthly, Not Seasonally Adjusted

Figure 11.4 Gold Price and Consumer Confidence.
Source: ICE Benchmark Administration

What does the behavior of these two series during periods of recession tell you about the influence of confidence on gold prices?

6. Compare and contrast two to three ways in which shares of stocks act differently as an investment, as compared with gold.

7. Explain how operating under a gold standard may prevent the Federal Reserve from stimulating an economy during a recession. Specify what the Fed would like to do with monetary policy and interest rates, and what they are actually able to do.

8. Suppose a foreign trading partner decides to leave the gold standard and raises their interest rate.

   a. Using a foreign exchange market diagram, show what the domestic country must do with their interest rate in order to keep the exchange rate fixed.

   b. What happened to the central bank's supply of reserves in the process, and can this cause instability in the exchange rate regime?

12 Cryptocurrencies

Objectives

1. To learn what a cryptocurrency is and whether or not it is "money."
2. A very brief overview of the concept of a "blockchain" is presented.

Cryptocurrency, a word never heard of until just a few short years ago, now has become a mainstream topic, found in the news, social media, and daily conversations of millions of people around the globe. It has truly captured the imagination and has become nothing short of a phenomenon. But what is it, and what is its worth, and what is its future? This chapter focuses primarily on the economic possibilities of cryptocurrency and will not dig deeply into its technical makeup, as that can be researched more deeply on the web.

The basics of cryptocurrency

Just what is cryptocurrency? Well, it is a computer algorithm that was developed a few years ago. The first cryptocurrency was called Bitcoin and it is still the best known of all the cryptocurrencies. Other examples include: Litecoin, Ripple, Ethereum, Dogecoin, and Coinye. It only exists in computers, recorded on a digital ledger of sorts, called a *blockchain*. Most digital currencies are of limited issue, with a finite number of available coins stated at creation and built into the blockchain software.

Cryptocurrencies, such as Bitcoin, are issued, or mined, by players all over the world who compete to find a very complex solution to a computer-generated mathematical problem. The first computer to solve the problem is designated as the computer to open the next block in the blockchain and is awarded a predetermined amount of digital currency. All of the computers who are running the ledger software then update accordingly and the entire process begins again. A new block is added to the blockchain about every 10 minutes. The system is quite effective, with the reward providing incentive for miners to continue competing to solve the problems, and the constantly generated updates providing almost impenetrable security.

The process is very energy intensive, so these rigorous computer calculations are mostly done in areas with abundant, cheap electricity. Still, the

DOI: 10.4324/9781003251453-15

cost can run into the hundreds of thousands of dollars annually. This creates a barrier to entry for anyone thinking they can just boot up a computer and begin mining for digital currency. However, those who are familiar with coding and have the means to get into the business can find it quite lucrative, as miners are paid in digital currency at a more than nominal rate. For example, in May 2021, the reward for a bitcoin miner who solves a problem was 6.25 bitcoins. The recipient of the coins may hold them, offer them for sale on the market at the current price, or trade them for goods and services. These rewards are granted each time a problem is solved, with the rate of reward continuing for a preset period of time, about 4 years, before being reduced by 50%. The halving will continue indefinitely until 21 billion bitcoins have been issued, at which time no new coins may be mined.

As mentioned, all digital currencies are traded through a program called blockchain, which is a computer linked, distributed, and decentralized system maintained on the computers of all users who are running the blockchain program. It acts as a permanent ledger that records all digital currency transactions as well as a super secure system designed to transmit virtually any kind of data. Because there is no single computer or server responsible for maintaining the blockchain, it lives as long as there is an internet connection to any single computer running the software, therefore it is basically impossible to shut it down without wiping out the entire internet. This technology offers potential for an unlimited number of applications and many companies are developing their own blockchain systems for moving data more quickly and securely than ever before possible. These individually created systems do not yet share standards for interlinking with other blockchains, but standards are likely to emerge in the not-too-distant future to allow greater connectivity and nearly impenetrable security. The authors of this textbook believe that blockchain technology and its continued development may present more true lasting value than digital currency itself.

Is cryptocurrency money?

While the publicity and excitement for Bitcoin, and other similar coins, get attention, its drawbacks are considerable. We must consider the role of digital currency in our economy. Is it money? According to the definition that we outlined earlier, money must fulfill three main functions: it must provide a medium of exchange, it must act as a store of value, and it must serve as a unit of account. While digital coins may provide one or two of these functions in certain circumstances, none of them adequately supplies all three.

Can digital coins provide a medium of exchange? The idea of a digital payment is nothing new and the suggestion of being able to use digital coins to transact business in all areas of our lives is certainly compelling. At the present time, the use of cryptocurrency to make routine purchases, such as walking into a local hardware store to purchase a hammer and some nails, is limited. This is primarily because most retail stores, especially smaller ones, are not set up to accept it as payment. Since cryptocurrency is only stored digitally, a shopper who wishes to use it to purchase an item must have a means to transfer the coin from their account, or digital wallet, to that of the seller. There are several platforms that were designed for business use, specifically providing retailers with the technology to receive payments in digital currency. There are some significant limitations to these platforms, including speed (they are typically too slow for use with in-person, register-based transactions) and lack of uniformity (each platform may only operate with one particular variety of cryptocurrency), but those problems will likely be worked out as market demand grows. Some well-known companies, such as Microsoft, Home Depot, Overstock, Starbucks, and Whole Foods, are early adopters of these platforms and now accept forms of cryptocurrency as payment for online or app-based purchases. A few sports franchises are beginning to accept digital currency for online sales of game tickets. Some fast-food restaurants are getting into the cryptocurrency game in larger markets. With app-based services, such as Door Dash, Uber, and others, becoming more mainstream, it is likely that digital currencies will eventually be useful for routine purchases.

Is cryptocurrency a store of value? Can a digital coin that you hold today be used to purchase a new Microsoft product next month? Yes, but only assuming Microsoft is willing to accept it as payment. Since many companies do not yet accept cryptocurrency and there are multiple coins on the market with more likely to come, your coin may not be accepted at the retailer of your choice. Further, you must accept the risk presented by the volatility of cryptocurrency values. While inflation must be factored in, we still understand the nominal measurement of the dollar. That cannot be said of cryptocurrencies, as their values fluctuate and there is no guarantee that a unit held today will be honored as the same unit of measure tomorrow. And it may not be honored at all, as the value of digital currency rests on the assumption that others will accept it as payment or in exchange for other currencies. The lack of stability works against this, making cryptocurrency a questionable store of value.

Can cryptocurrency act as a reliable unit of account? This means that it would serve as a common base for price comparison between products or services. With multiple cryptocurrencies on the market and highly volatile values, this requirement is relatively more elusive. Quoting the price of a shirt in dollars makes it easily understandable and you can compare prices between retailers. On the other hand, cryptocurrencies are each denominated in their own units of account. So, if the price of a shirt is quoted in bitcoin, you must understand that it could be highly volatile and comparison with other retailers would only be possible if their advertised prices are also expressed in bitcoin. Further, with multiple digital currencies in use, you could be faced with comparing apples to oranges, so to speak. At the end of the day, users will likely need to covert cryptocurrency values to some reliable measure, such as dollars, underscoring the limitations for cryptocurrency as a unit of account.

Unlike the U.S. dollar, the British pound, the Japanese yen, etc., digital coins do not have the backing of a sovereign issuer, therefore they are not universally useful as a medium of exchange. They can store value, but that value is not consistent and the inherent volatility erodes confidence in their future purchasing power. With multiple digital coins on the market and limited acceptance of each, cryptocurrency is a poor unit of account. What is the root of the limitations we just discussed? In each case, cryptocurrencies' less-than-optimum ability to meet the requirements to function as money are related to the fact that they are not fiat currencies.

A discussion of cryptocurrency should consider the primary characteristics of money: durability (digital coins do not decay or otherwise deteriorate), portability (since cryptocurrencies are virtual assets, stored in digital wallets, they're highly portable), divisibility (digital coins can be divided into minute fractions), and availability (supply of each currency is finite but more can be developed). It is easy to see that digital currencies bear these characteristics fairly well, especially as compared to other assets such as gold, pebbles, spices, or any other things that have been used as money throughout history. However, for any currency to truly have lasting utility, its nominal liquidity must be dependable. If we deposit a dollar into a bank account today, we know that we will be able to make a withdrawal and receive a dollar in cash at any point in the future. With a digital currency, such as Bitcoin, we cannot be certain as to the amount we will receive, if any, when we decide to liquidate.

For many of us, the idea of digital currency is compelling. We might appreciate the convenience of it or be compelled by the ease, speed, and anonymity with which we can transfer it. If we own a small business, we could enjoy the ability to conduct transactions with anyone, anywhere, without the time and expense of visiting a bank or paying wire transfer fees. All of those things certainly make life easier. However, for many around the world, cryptocurrency could open up brand new opportunities. Since anyone with a computer or cell phone can operate a digital wallet, virtual currency creates the means for asset-based exchanges rather than account-based transactions, serving as a cash alternative for those who choose not to use commercial banks. With some minimal infrastructure, it may allow lesser developed areas of the world to access resources and increase productivity. Of course, this would all require common platforms or apps and more ubiquitous acceptance, but that may not be far down the road.

Certainly, there is great potential for the utility of Bitcoin and other cryptocurrencies. However, there are hurdles to overcome before we would see widespread adoption of digital currency in its present form. Currently, it is believed that many coin transactions are used for tax evasion schemes and for money laundering. While this is mostly due to the mystique associated with the fact that it is a virtual asset, the lack of transparency does lend suspicion. Proponents hail the anonymity of cryptocurrency and that hallmark undeniably provides fertile ground for corruption. But, rest assured, the government is well aware of this weakness and at some point regulators will find a way to implement oversight and end this use.

Indeed, tax authorities are already at the forefront of regulating crypto-currency transactions. From a tax perspective, digital currency is treated like any other property investment. Because it is not backed by any govern-ment body, digital currency is still valued in terms of fiat currency. There-fore, sales or exchanges are taxed just like stocks, bonds, or even gold. If you purchased 1 Bitcoin (BTC) on January 1st for $40,000 and sell it on June 15th for $70,000, this would result in a $30,000 taxable short-term capital gain. Gain would also be triggered if you used that Bitcoin to buy a car, just as it would if you liquidated a stock to make the purchase. While all of this is well-understood by accountants and tax preparers, it is suspected that many taxable transactions go unreported. Because the previously mentioned ano-nymity makes it difficult to implement systematic reporting standards, there is opportunity for misuse without much chance of repercussion.

As stated earlier, the vast majority of digital currency is held for pure spec-ulation. Like any other investment, values fluctuate with the market. The vol-atility of cryptocurrency makes it especially appealing to short-term traders who are already well experienced in using digital platforms for speculative trades. The asset may be new but the pattern is the same: as more players enter the market and push prices higher, a certain euphoric high sets in, and this momentum continues, until it doesn't...consider the following figure (Figure 12.1) that displays the average monthly price of Bitcoin over time.

The behavior of the price of Bitcoin in 2020–2021 certainly exhibits bubble-like behavior. On March 12, 2020, the price was $4980, and a little over a year later on April 15, 2021, the price was $63,347, which was a 1172 percentage increase! In some sense, this is not that unlike the tulip bulb

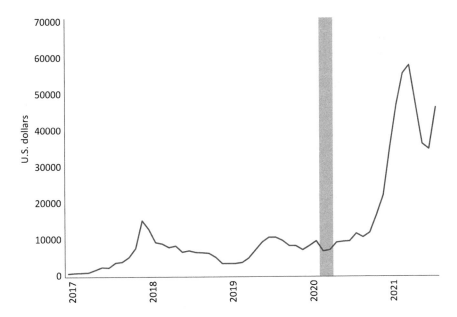

Figure 12.1 Bitcoin Price.
Source: Coinbase

bubble that occurred in the Netherland in the 1630s, where the price of a common tulip bulb rose from 1 guilder in January 1637 to 30 guilders by February 1637. In other words, both assets saw astronomical and inexplicable increases in price over an extremely short period of time.

Ultimately, an asset settles at a price in the market that reflects its true utility in our lives. But at the time of this writing, it's value is not reliable or sustainable over time, as it is not backed by anything of fundamental value.

What does the future hold?

Will cryptocurrencies become money, equal to that issued by governments? Many people want that to happen as they have a basic distrust of government and believe money creation should be privatized. However, they miss the point that we discussed in Chapter 4. The key component of money creation is the credit that is created when a new loan is made. This happens inside the banking system, constrained by market demand, and it only works when the currency has a sovereign issuer. Because digital coins do not have a sovereign issuer, they do not play a role in credit creation. Yes, you can borrow or lend digital coins, but you are simply shifting assets back and forth. Nothing new has been created. No new credit is being issued and the money supply does not expand. The amount of each new digital currency is usually predetermined and finite and, with no government backing, its value is determined by the market. In its current form, adoption of cryptocurrency as 'real' money would be quite like operating on a gold standard, with all of the limitations that we have already discussed.

Certainly, digital currencies do represent purchasing power, which for many is the only meaningful aspect of money. Critics point out that, if the public at large came to believe cryptocurrency to be true money, it would encourage the uncontrolled creation of additional digital currencies. They believe that more and more cryptocurrency creators could vastly increase the amount of 'money' in the global economy, leading to long-term inflation and other problems. While it is possible, even probable, that the number of digital currencies in circulation will continue to grow, we must remember that as long as they are not tied to any central bank, they will still be property, just like stocks or bonds. Without the backing of a sovereign currency, they are not fiat money, and they are not issued through the banking system. While they are initially released through mining, digital coins are generally acquired by purchase, meaning that holders pay for them with either sovereign currency or, perhaps, with another digital currency which was purchased with sovereign currency. They simply represent the velocity of money already outstanding. This is comparable to gold. Mining companies may extract the gold but it only makes its way to investors by way of sale or exchange. Therefore, the mere existence of additional cryptocurrencies would generally be no more inflationary than any other form of investment product. However, the existence of other units of account can be disruptive to the monetary system; thus, there are reasons for caution as long as digital currencies in circulation continue to grow.

Cryptocurrency advocates often hail the fact that digital currencies operate independently, outside of the commercial banking system. For those who do not trust the government or big corporations, having an independent currency seems ideal. They take aim at the ability of central banks to manipulate the money supply and finance rampant government spending. Having a peer-to-peer network in charge of the currency system, they argue, would eliminate that control and allow users worldwide to operate on a more even playing field.

For those who understand the job of a central bank, the idea of moving away from fiat currency is especially troublesome, as wide acceptance of cryptocurrency as a unit of account could render central bank monetary policy less effective. Central banks rely heavily on open market operations to regulate the economy. They lean on rate setting to fine tune monetary policies as needed to control inflation and manage credit creation. This all happens through interaction with the commercial banking system and by virtue of the fact that the primary unit of account is sovereign currency. Therefore, central bank policies can only impact central bank denominated currencies. This connection is lost if cryptocurrency becomes widely accepted as an alternate unit of account and the interest rates set by the central bank would no longer have the same impact on interest rates or inflation in the overall economy.

Many of the world's leading economists believe that major central banks will unite to combat uncontrolled cryptocurrency and that global legislation will be passed to control its use while also developing ways to harness its benefits. Currently, it appears that the U.S. Federal Reserve and other major central banks are coordinating a response to this concern. Much of the discussion is being conducted through the BIS (Bank for International Settlements), the institution mentioned earlier in this book. Since central banks are the primary agents deployed by governments to manage their economies, they are naturally keeping a close watch on developments in the world of cryptocurrencies. The key to implementing and maintaining monetary policies is the monopolistic control that is vested in the central bank. If that power is threatened by unregulated currencies, the ability to fine tune the economy is weakened. Therefore, the chance that major governments would ever accept a digital currency, such as bitcoin, and back it as a legitimate currency, is remote.

The far more likely scenario is the offering of a digital version of currency already in circulation. In fact, we know that the U.S. Federal Reserve (and presumably other major central banks, as well) is considering the idea of a government-issued cryptocurrency. We can assume that this new 'Fed Coin' would be denominated in dollars and be tradeable only on digital platforms. Essentially, it would be another form of currency in circulation, providing an alternative to cash that would be held in digital wallets. Because it would have the government backing, it would bear all of the characteristics of money. And since we can presume it would operate on widespread digital platforms, it could be available to users who choose to be unbanked. Critics say that this would lead to individual users being able to transact business directly through the central bank, bypassing the commercial banking system. But, as we know, the central bank is not in the business of making loans. And because most currency exists in the form of deposits, rather than currency in circulation, the banking system would never be eliminated. Thus, by adding a digital element to the currency circulating throughout the economy, the new digital currency would enhance what is already in place—it would improve transaction speed, improve efficiency throughout global banking systems, and replace much of the physical cash used today, all while saving money (as the production of coins is expensive). Viewed in this way, it seems inevitable.

Predictions for the future

The world of cryptocurrencies is a new area that has garnered a lot of attention in recent years, and its story is incomplete. This following list summarizes what we know about cryptocurrencies at this moment in time:

- Blockchain will enable a much-improved sharing of secure information globally, improving living standards around the world.
- A digital wallet system will bring efficiency to the exchange and transfer of money throughout the world, improving lives.
- Cryptocurrencies are not 'money,' mainly because they do not provide a widely accepted medium of exchange. Instead, cryptocurrencies are a form of asset, and prices appear to exhibit bubble-like tendencies.

Key terms

- **Cryptocurrency**—a form of digital asset which is based on a network that is distributed across a large number of computers and is secured by cryptography.
- **Blockchain**—a system in which a record of transactions made in cryptocurrency are maintained across computers which are linked to each other in a peer-to-peer network.

End-of-chapter problems

1. Consider what an asset needs in order to function as 'money.'
   a. List the three functions it must fulfill and briefly explain what they mean.
   b. Which of the three functions do cryptocurrencies come closest to successfully fulfilling?

c. Which of the three functions do cryptocurrencies come furthest from matching?

2. For an asset to be considered a reliable form of money, there are certain characteristics that it should have.

   a. Explain the difference between the functions of money and the characteristics of money.
   b. What are some good characteristics of money that cryptocurrencies might have?

3. Do some research independently and briefly explain the differences between Bitcoin, Litecoin, and Ethereum.

4. Go to the St. Louis Federal Reserve's website and download data on the price of Bitcoin, Litecoin, and Ethereum since 2017.

   a. What happens when you plot all three lines on the same chart? Now move Bitcoin's price to be plotted on the right-axis and observe what happens. What does this show?
   b. Find the date after January 1, 2019, when all three cryptocurrencies reached their lowest and highest prices.
   c. Calculate the percentage change from the lowest to highest price for all three cryptocurrencies. How do they compare? Why are they similar or different?

Conclusion

Money represents many things to many people. Something that is a resource for some can be a burden to others. Many people make money a goal, doing whatever they can to obtain what they envision as the ultimate status symbol. Others strive to live simply, taking a view of money as a necessary means for survival, but little else. The majority of people probably fall somewhere in between, desiring enough wealth to provide security and peace of mind plus a cushion beyond that which allows them to partake in a few luxuries and indulgences.

For economists, and perhaps, now, the reader who has completed this journey through the nuts and bolts of the economy, money is most definitely a tool. The product of the banking system, it is the essential element that fuels everything else in the economic engine. Money is created endogenously within the private sector by virtue of the commercial banking system's loan creation process. Perhaps that is the single most important nugget to take away from this book; the way the banking system works. Whether you are an aspiring economist, a young business professional, a hopeful entrepreneur, or an individual who wants to better understand the world we live in, you will certainly benefit from having insight into how the credit creation process works. You will be a better investor if you can navigate the way the commercial banking system works in conjunction with the central bank and the government's finance ministry and anticipate the way their interplay will impact the markets. You will be a more informed voter if you understand the role that government plays in influencing the money supply, helping you to evaluate political candidates and their platforms without being swayed by sound bites and fear tactics. You will be a more astute consumer if you are able to understand market cycles and the factors that influence supply and demand. And all of these things combine to help you be a better citizen.

Understanding the economy does not need to be an arduous task. It really is quite simple. Economics is not pure science. It involves a healthy dose of psychology. Predicting reactions and motives of others is fundamental to seeing the whole picture. For most of the countries that are part of the global economy, it is as much about feelings and human nature as it is about business and government. At its most basic, it is about confidence; it's about

DOI: 10.4324/9781003251453-16

unleashing our *animal spirits*, as economists like to say. And that is as it should be in a free market economy within a democracy. Money is just a tool. The driver is the human spirit.

That brings us to the end of our macroeconomic journey. We hope that you have learned a few things and that you are inspired to continue to learn. Each of us is a part of the global economy and each of us has a right to understand what makes it tick.

Now, one last thought: In considering the balance between the public and private sectors and the equilibrium of the three pillars of the economy, let us recount an acronym that was introduced to one of us in graduate school. It was on the first day of a class taught by a PhD economist who we students all feared for his brilliance. It was an economic decision making and analysis class and we expected high-level math and all kinds of complicated formulas. The professor walked to the chalkboard and said, "I am going to write something on this board that is going to be the heart and center of my course for the entire semester." As we watched, he wrote the letters, in all caps,

T A N S T A A F L.

At the time, very few people had heard that acronym, so we were all watching in fear and anticipation as he looked at us, grinned, and wrote under the letters, "*There ain't no such thing as a free lunch.*" We all laughed with relief.

Other references (not cited in text)

Web references for specifically mentioned stories or quotations:

Wikipedia, The Free Encyclopedia. http://en.wikipedia.org/wiki/Joseph_P._
Kennedy,_Sr.

http://news.google.com/newspapers?nid=2206&dat=19850220&id=2J8mAAAAI-
BAJ&sjid=jwEGAAAAIBAJ&pg=4628,1203198

http://en.wikipedia.org/wiki/Monetarism

http://en.proverbia.net/citasautor.asp?autor=15810

http://wallstcheatsheet.com/business/economy/heres-what-warren-buffett-says-
about-gold-and-commodities.html/

http://www.theatlantic.com/business/archive/2013/12/why-economics-is-really-
called-the-dismal-science/282454/

Books:

MONEY: What It Is How It Works by William F. Hummel, iUniverse, Inc. 2007

Periodicals, articles and other published works:

McGraw Hill Financial. "Repeat After Me: Banks Cannot and Do Not Lend Out
Reserves." By Paul Sheard. 13 August 2013 www.standardandpoors.com/spf/
upload/Ratings_US/Repeat_After_Me_8_14_13.pdf

He, Dong (2018) "Monetary Policy in the Digital Age," *Finance & Development.*
https://www.imf.org/external/pubs/ft/fandd/2018/06/central-bank-monetary-
policy-and-cryptocurrencies/he.pdf

Kenaga, Nicholas (2012) "Causes and Implications of the U.S. Housing Crisis," *The
Park Place Economist*: Vol. 20. http://digitalcommons.iwu.edu/parkplace/vol20/
iss1/12

Index

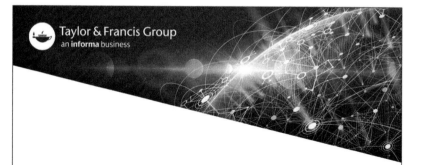